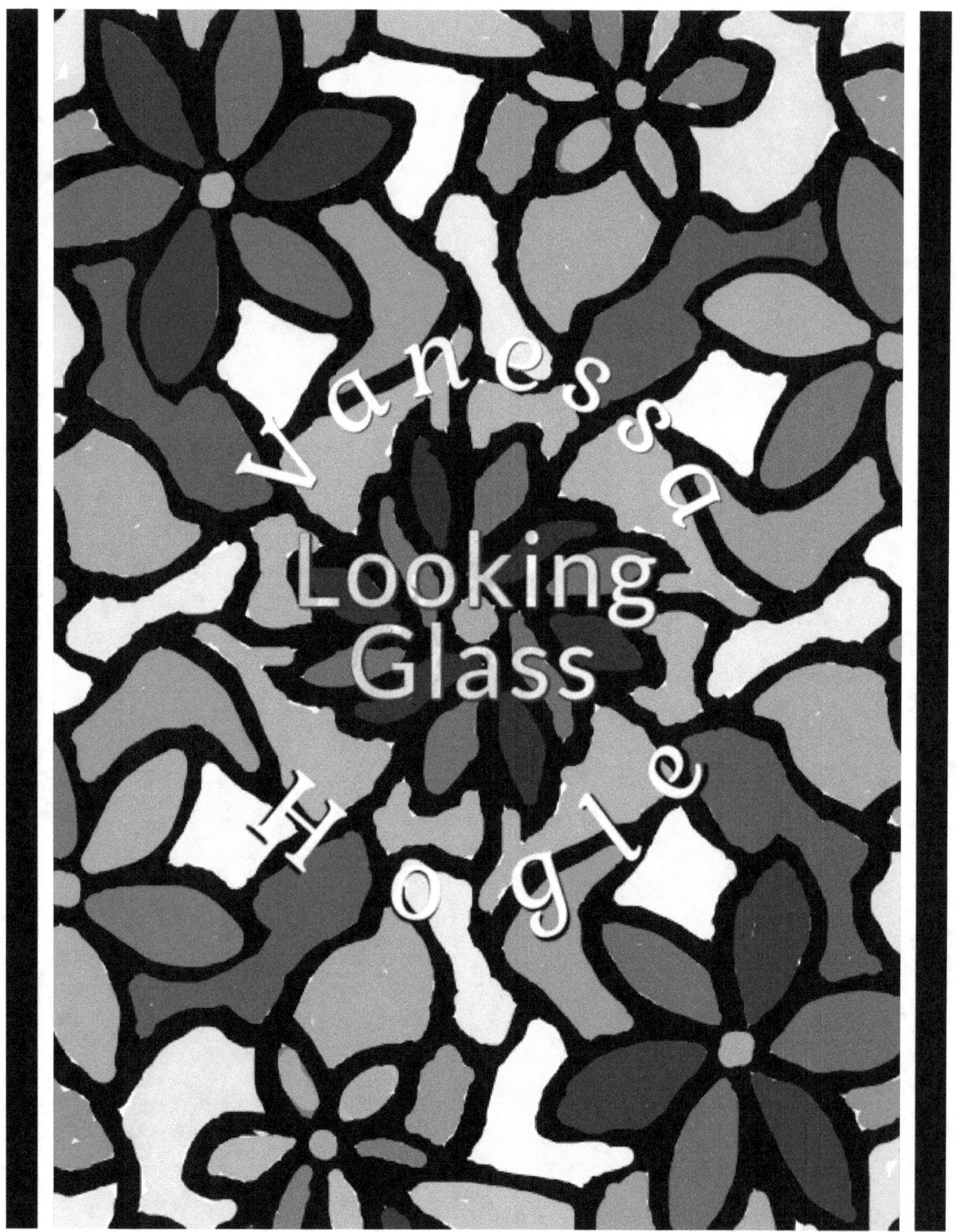

Vanessa
Looking
Glass
Hogle

First Edition
First Printing

Published by Perfect Trust Productions, LLC

www.perfecttrrustproductions.com

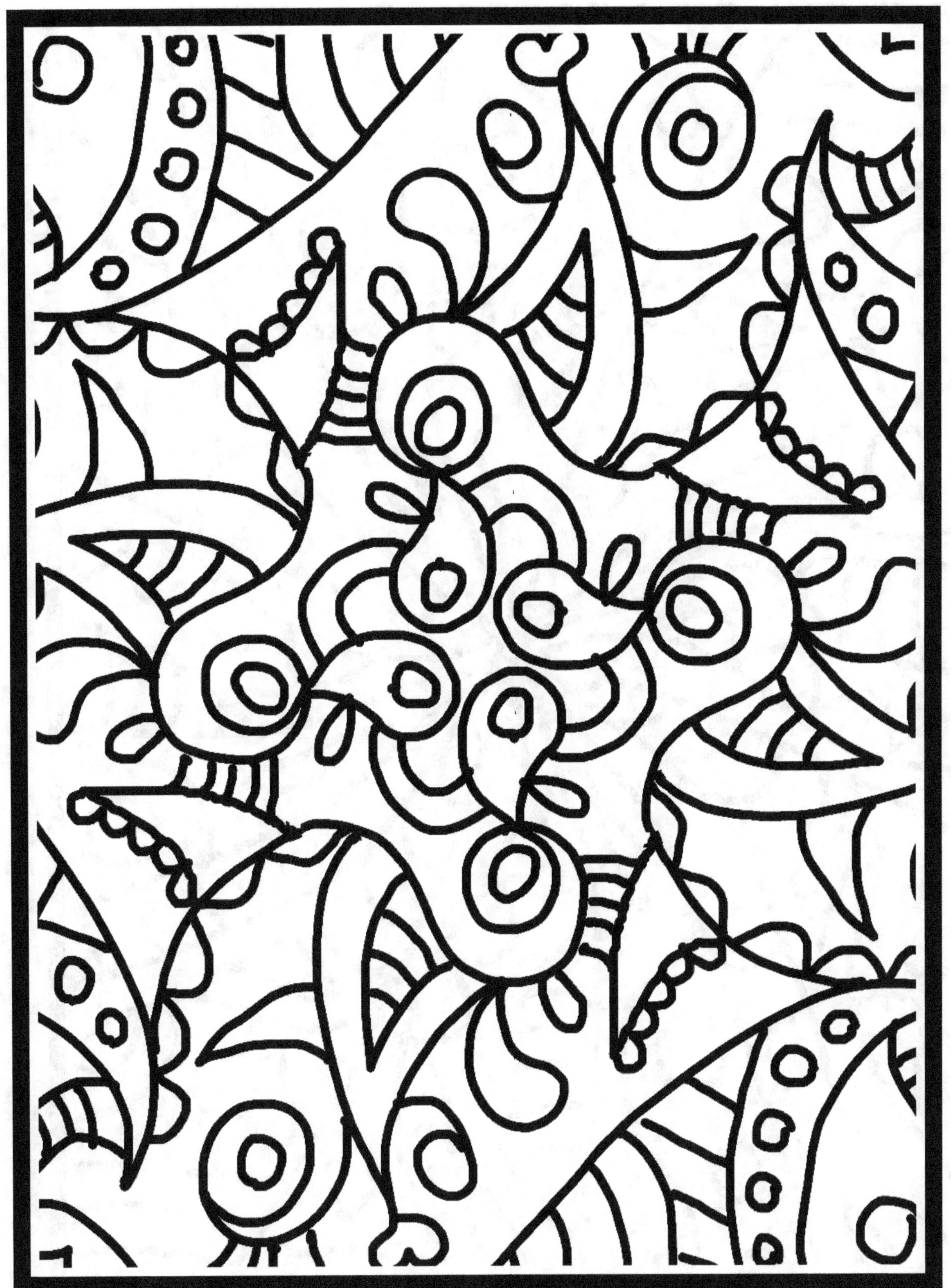

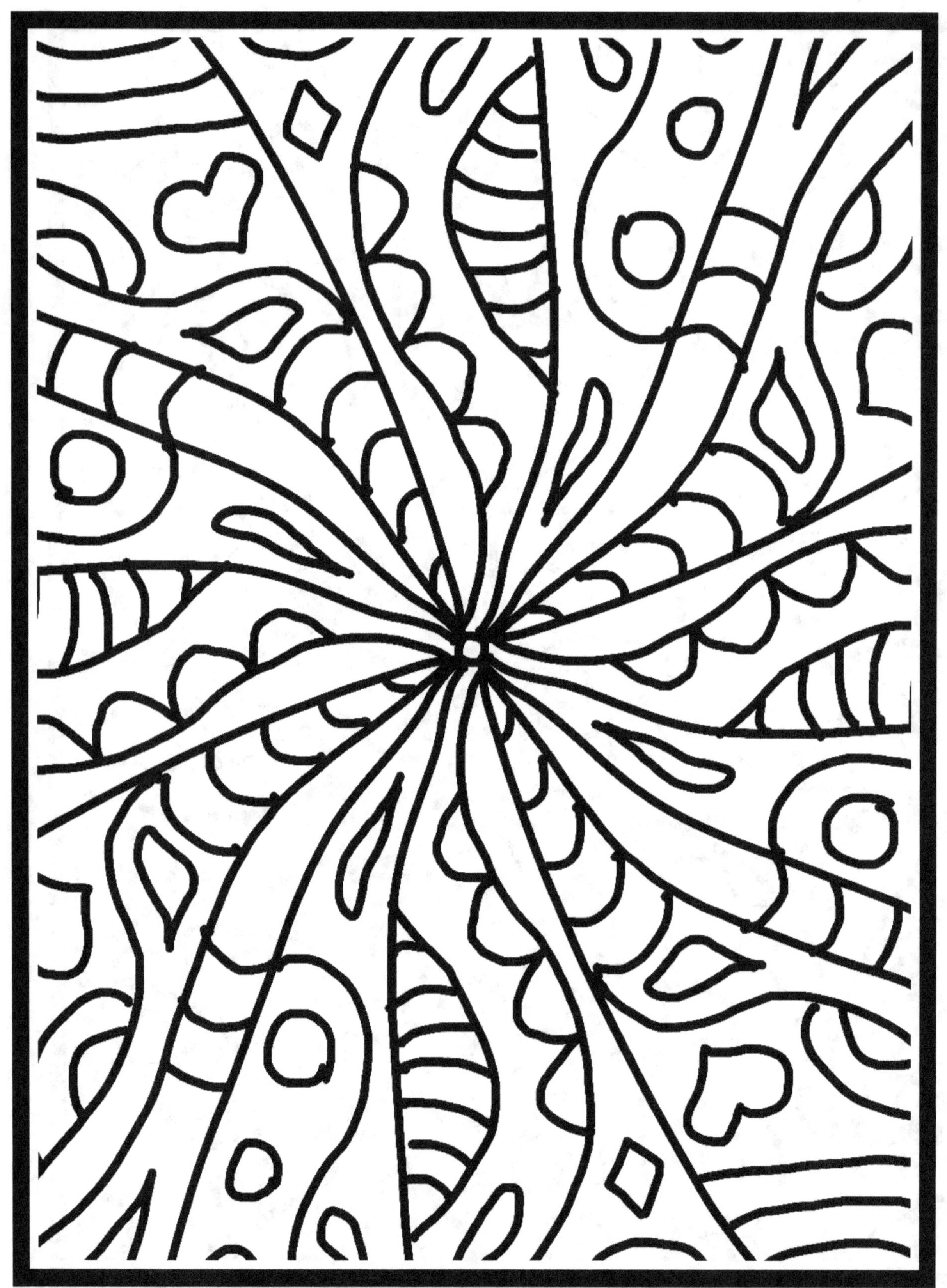

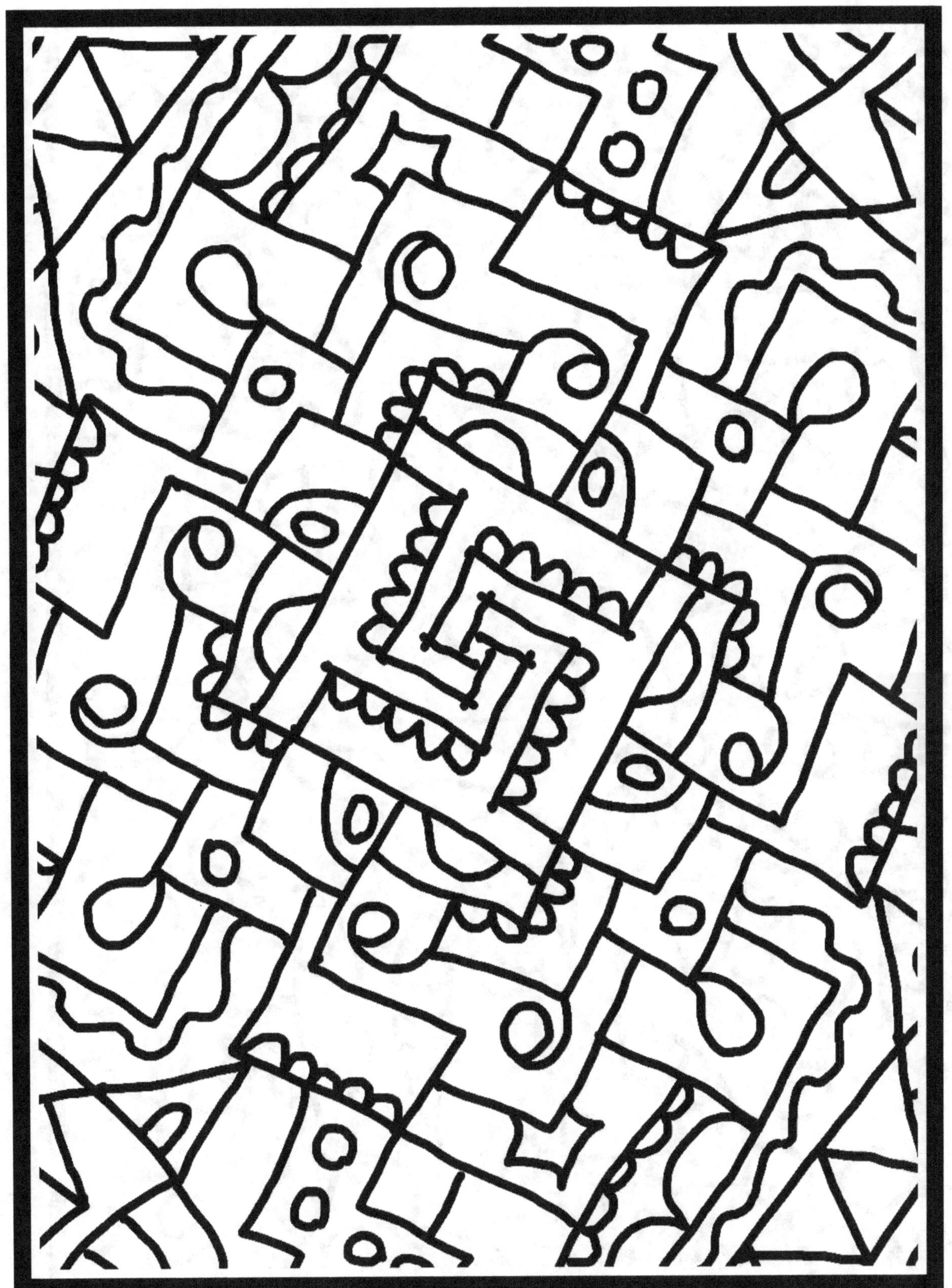

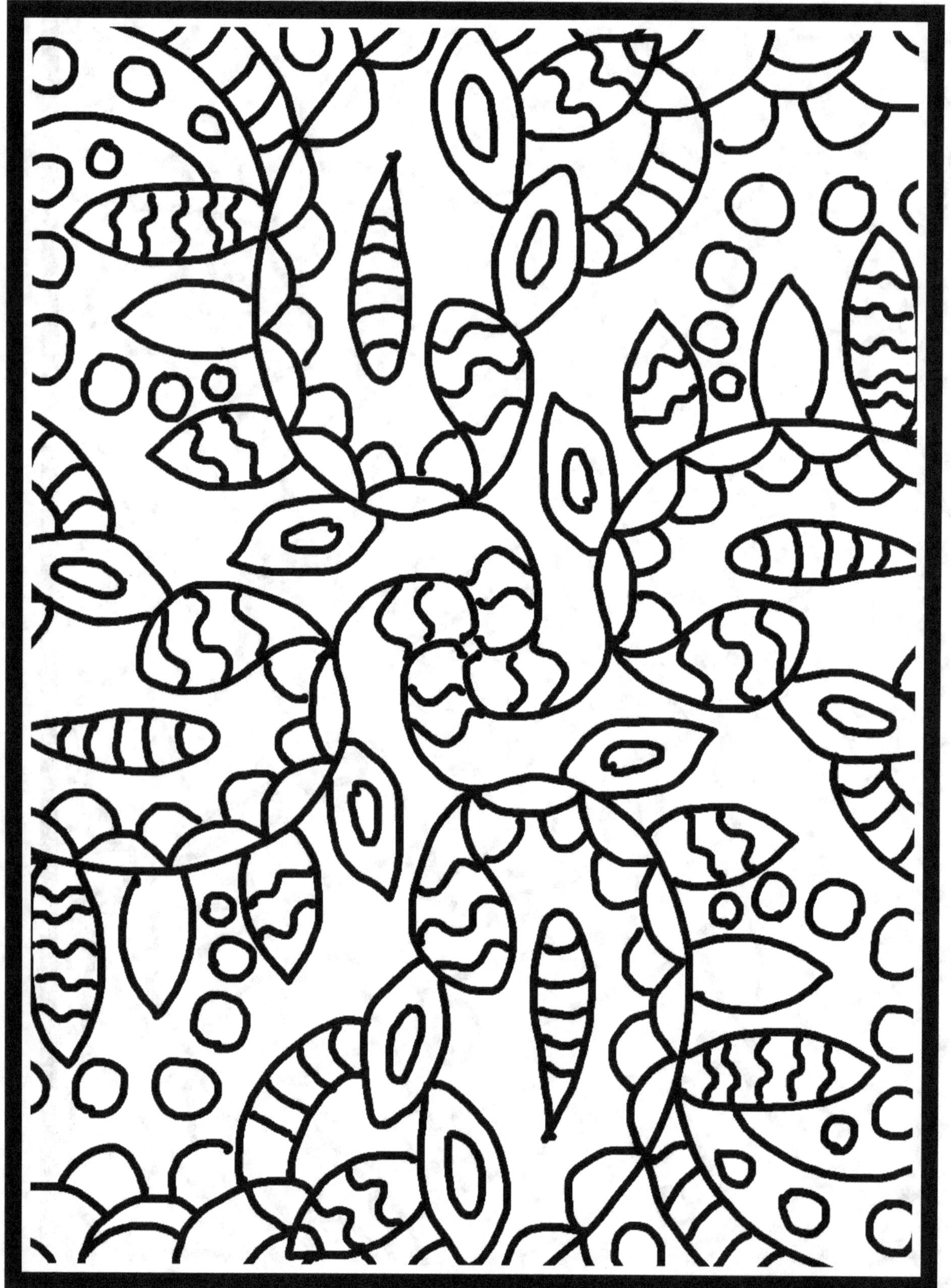

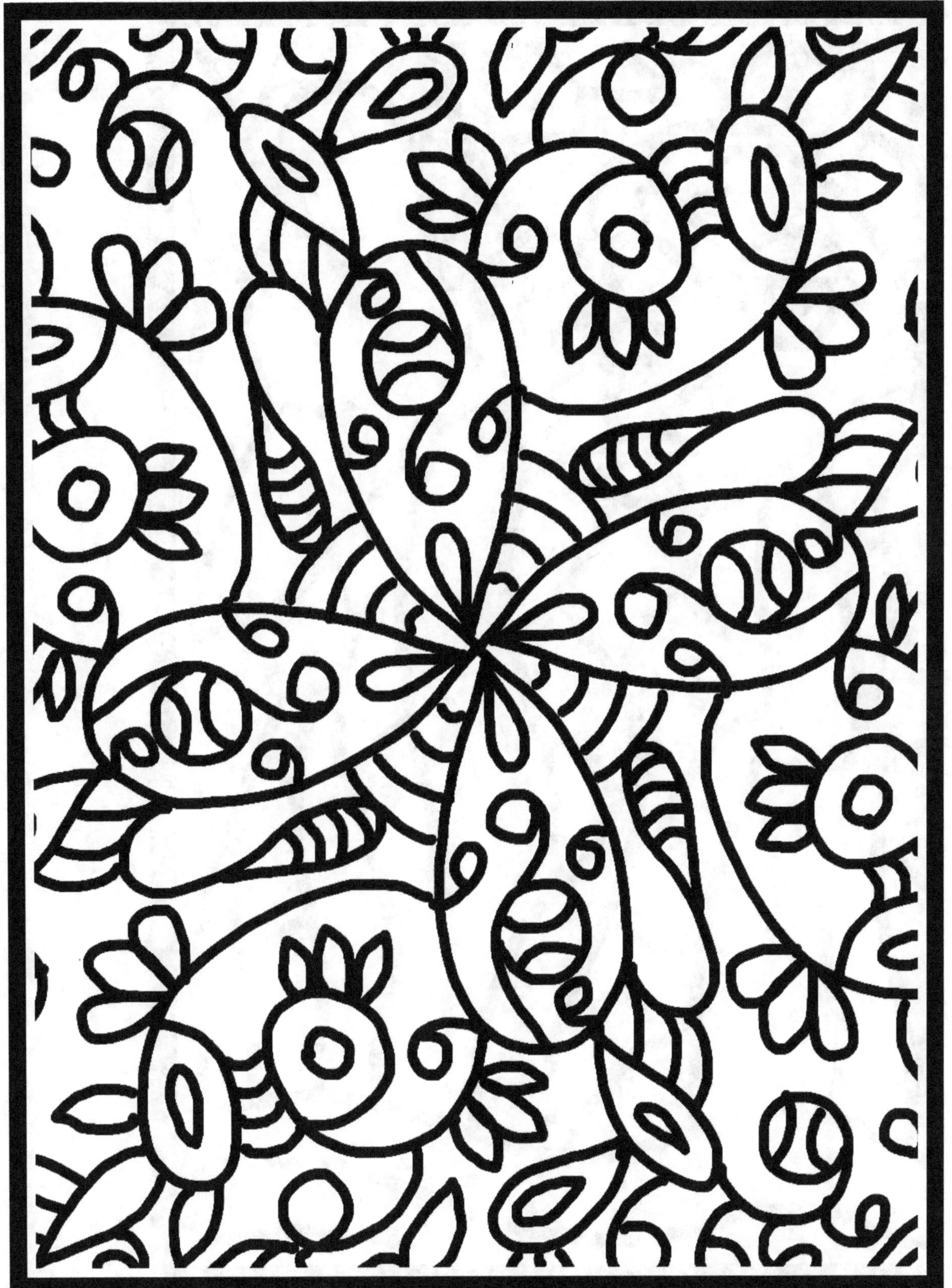

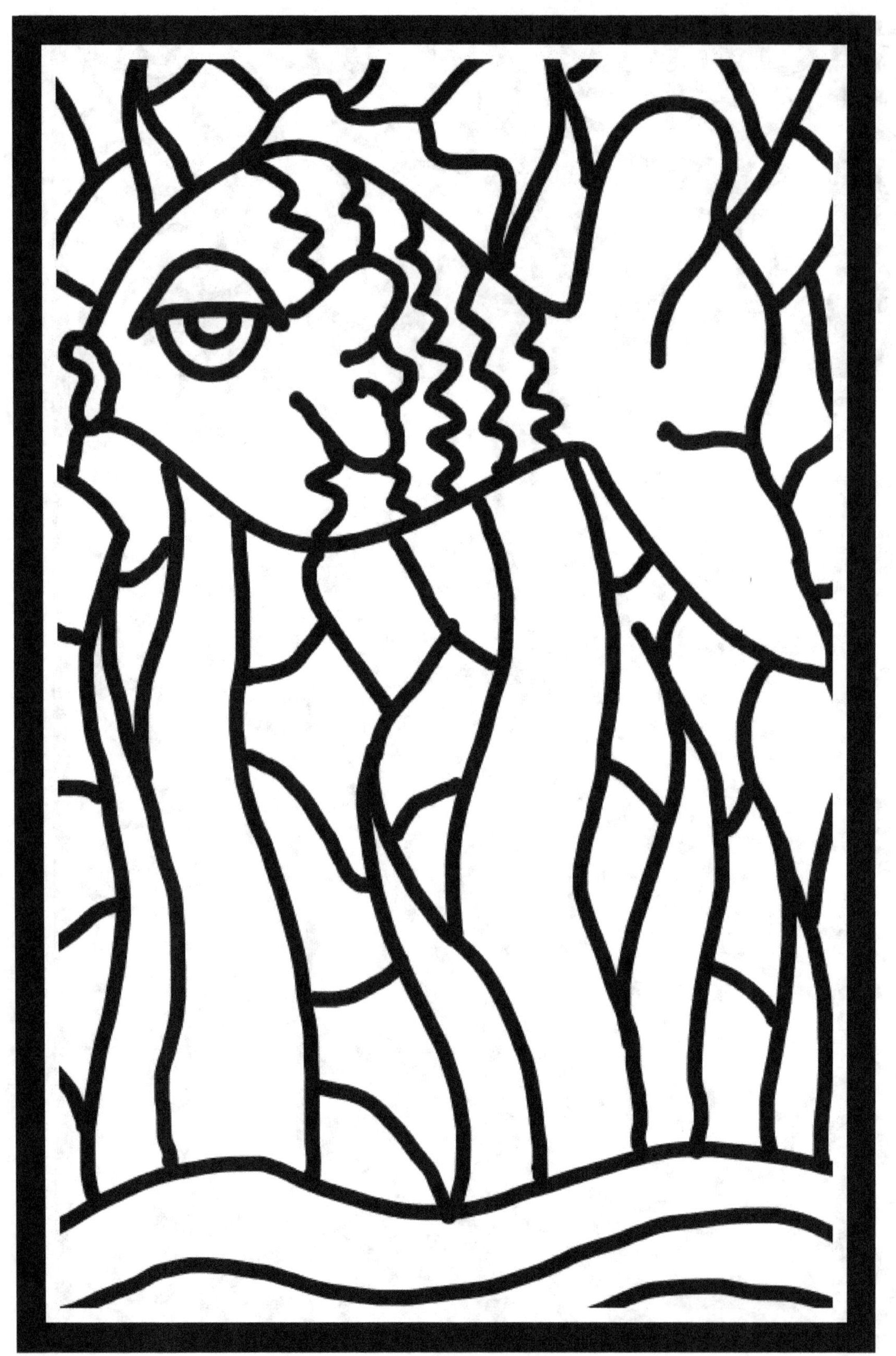

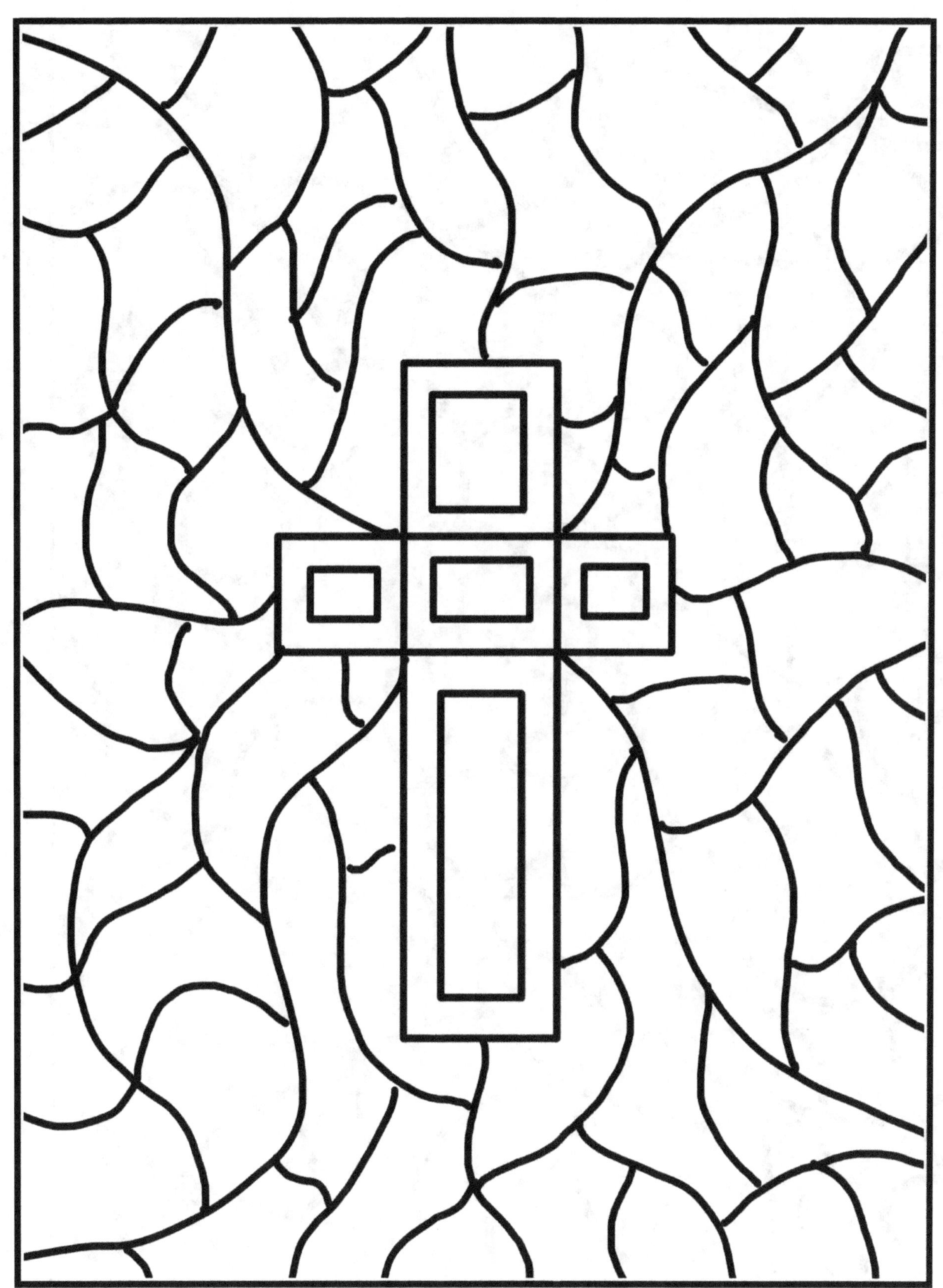

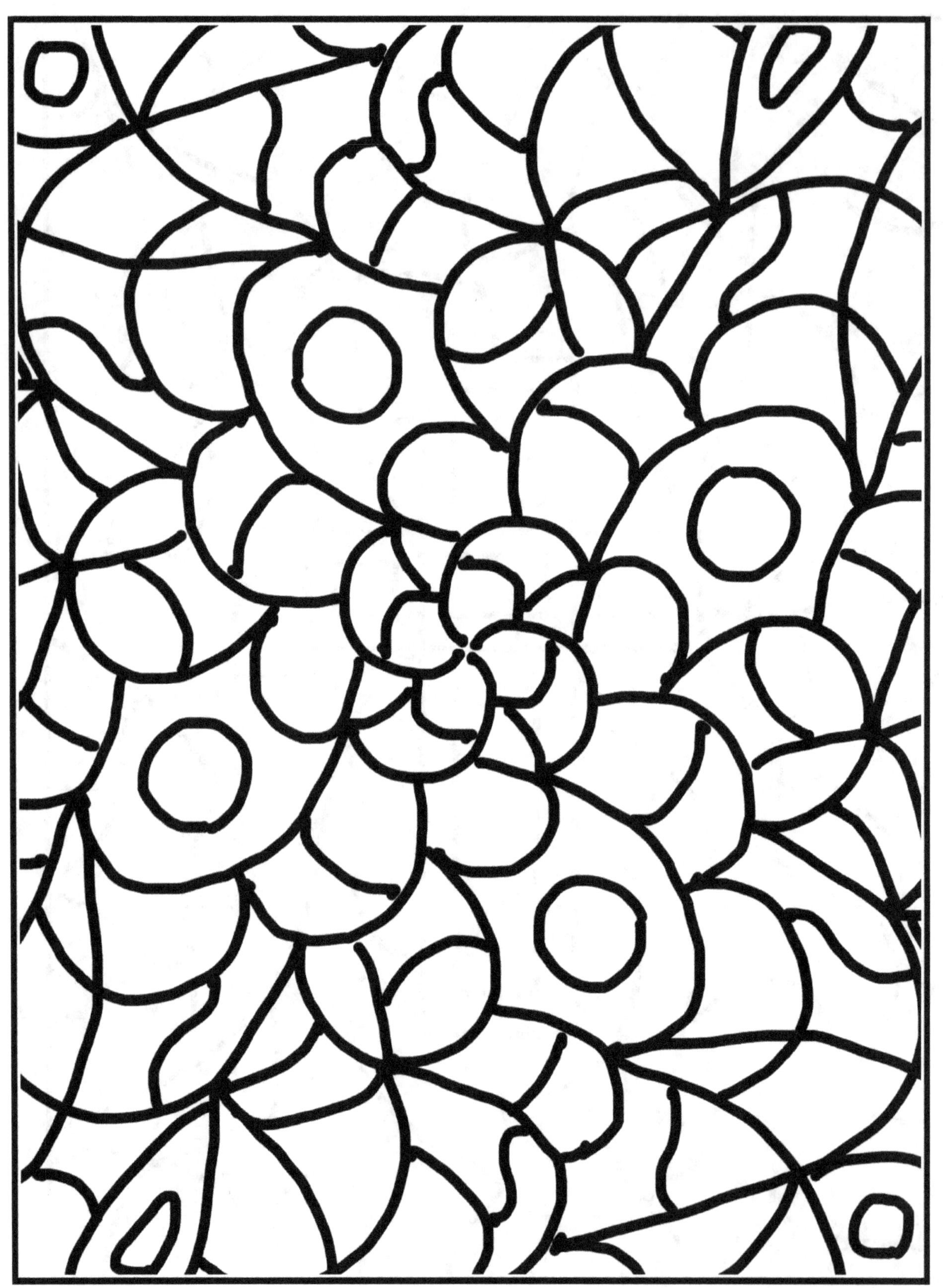

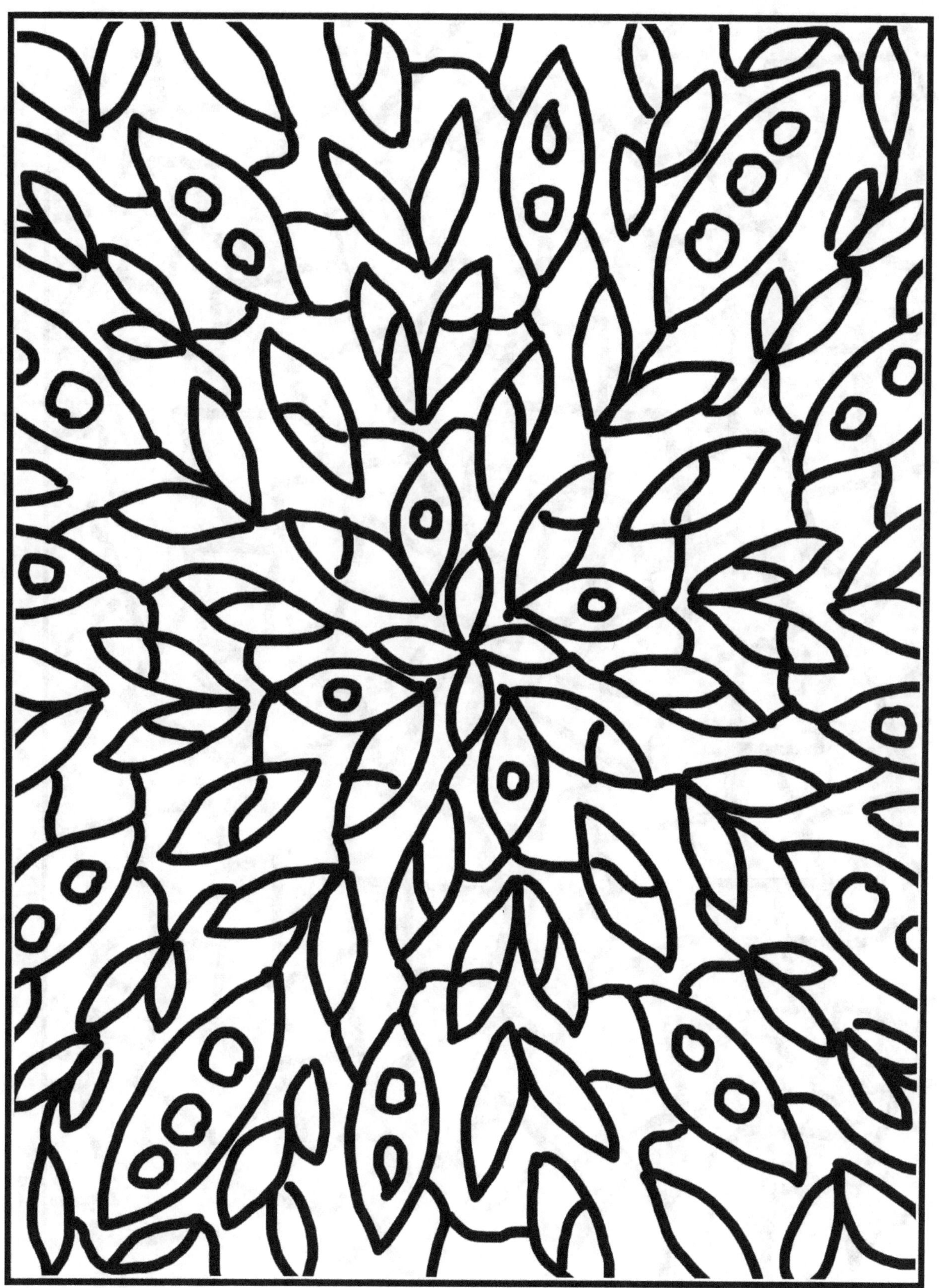

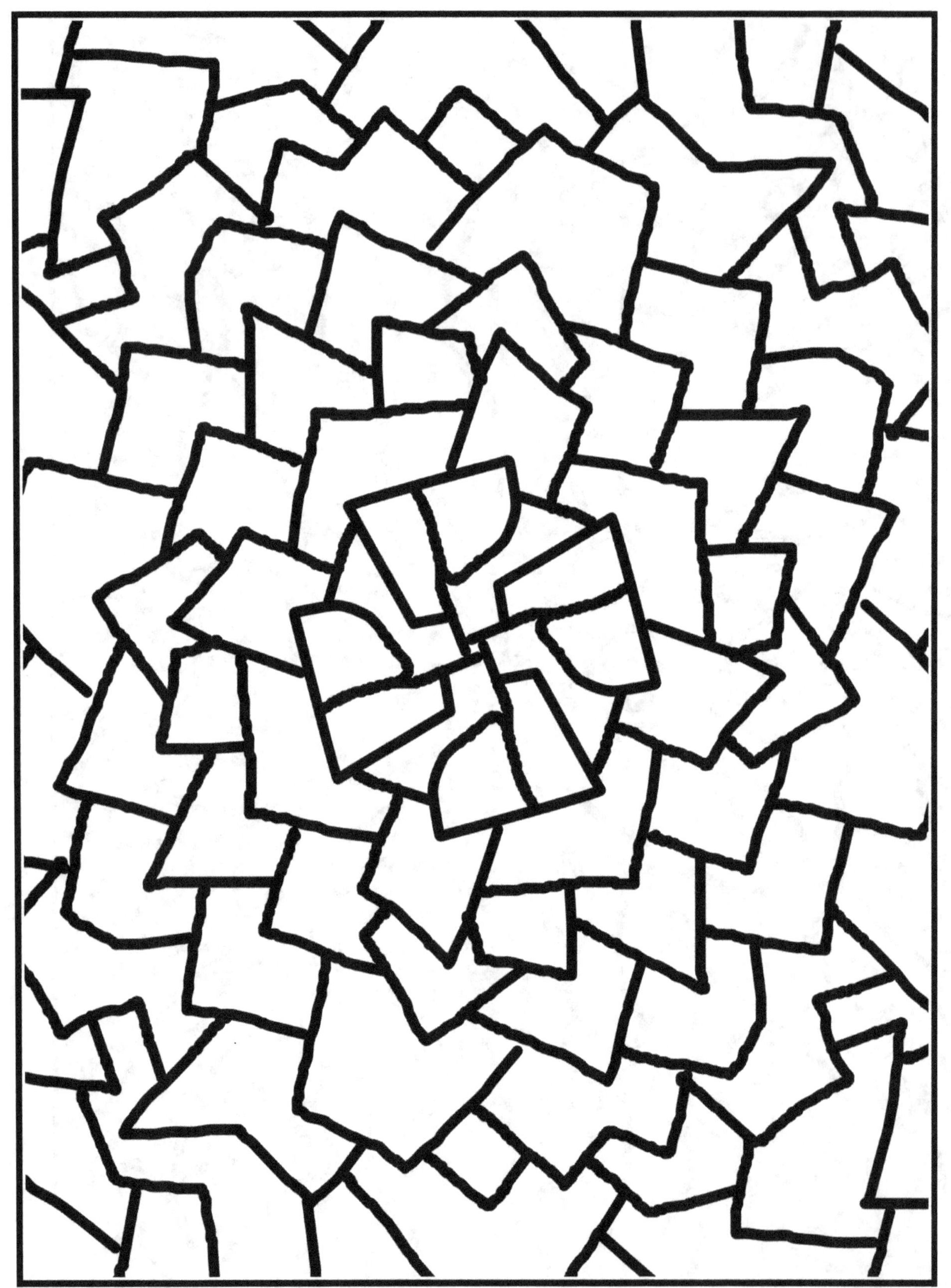

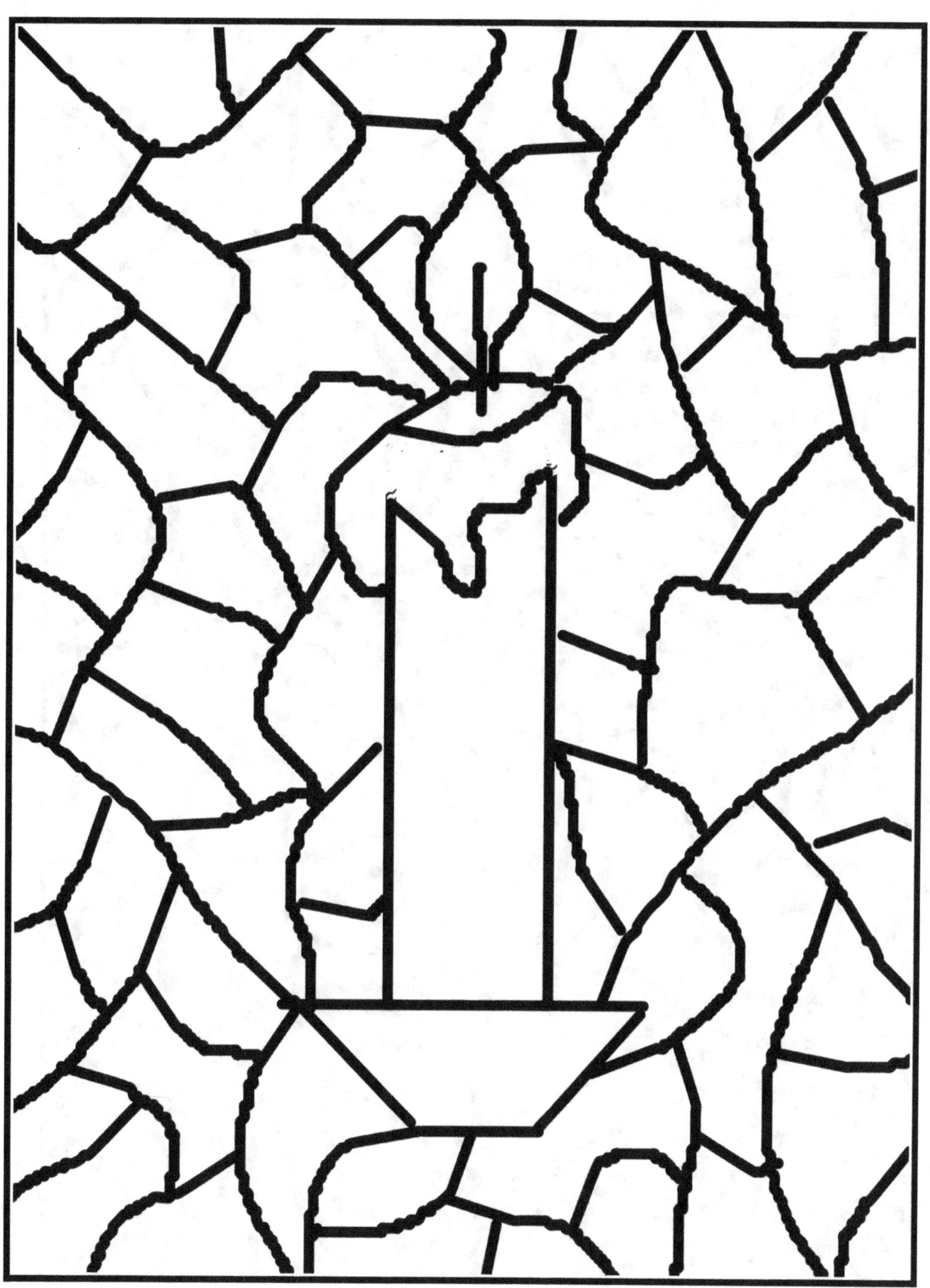

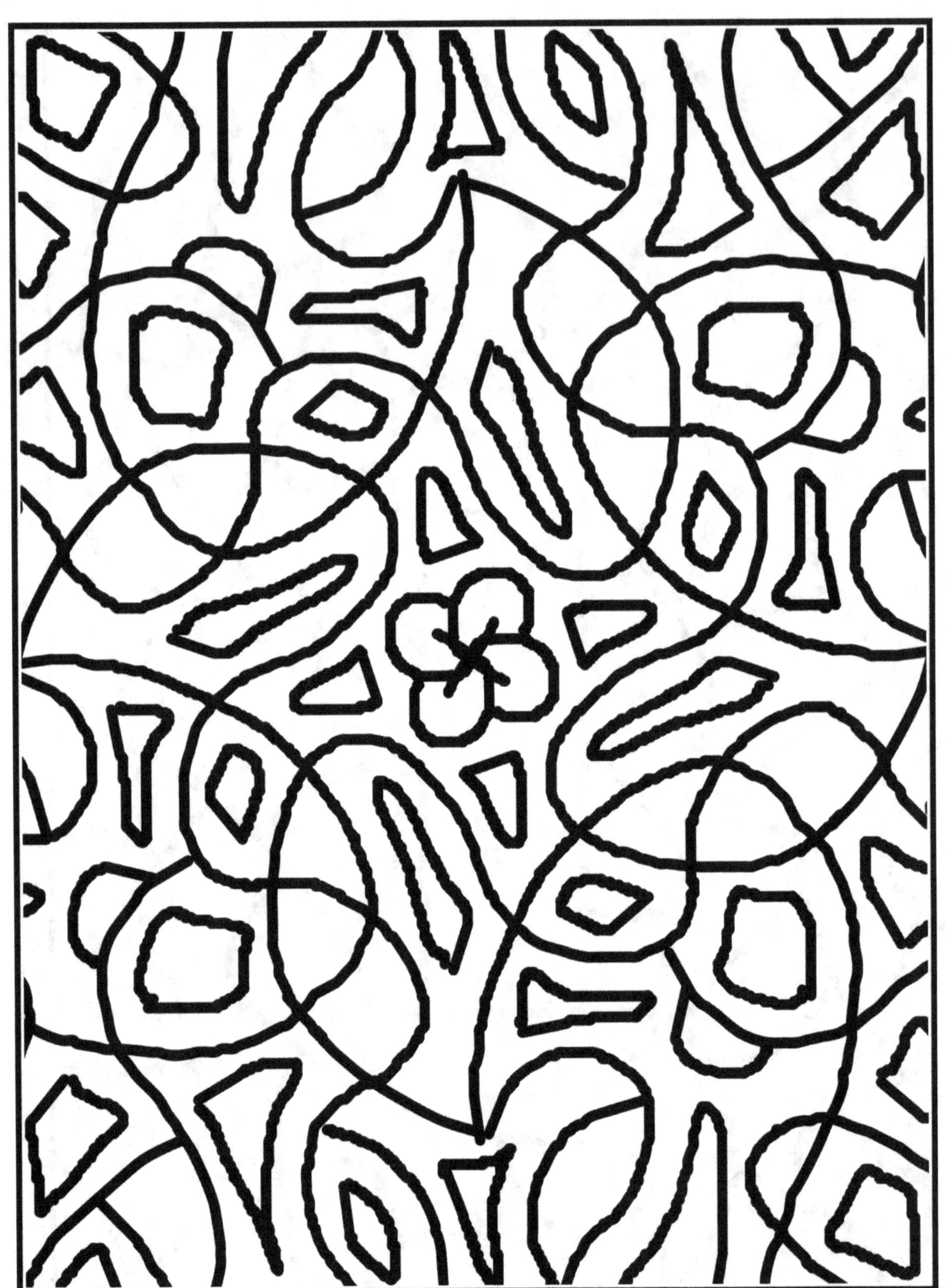

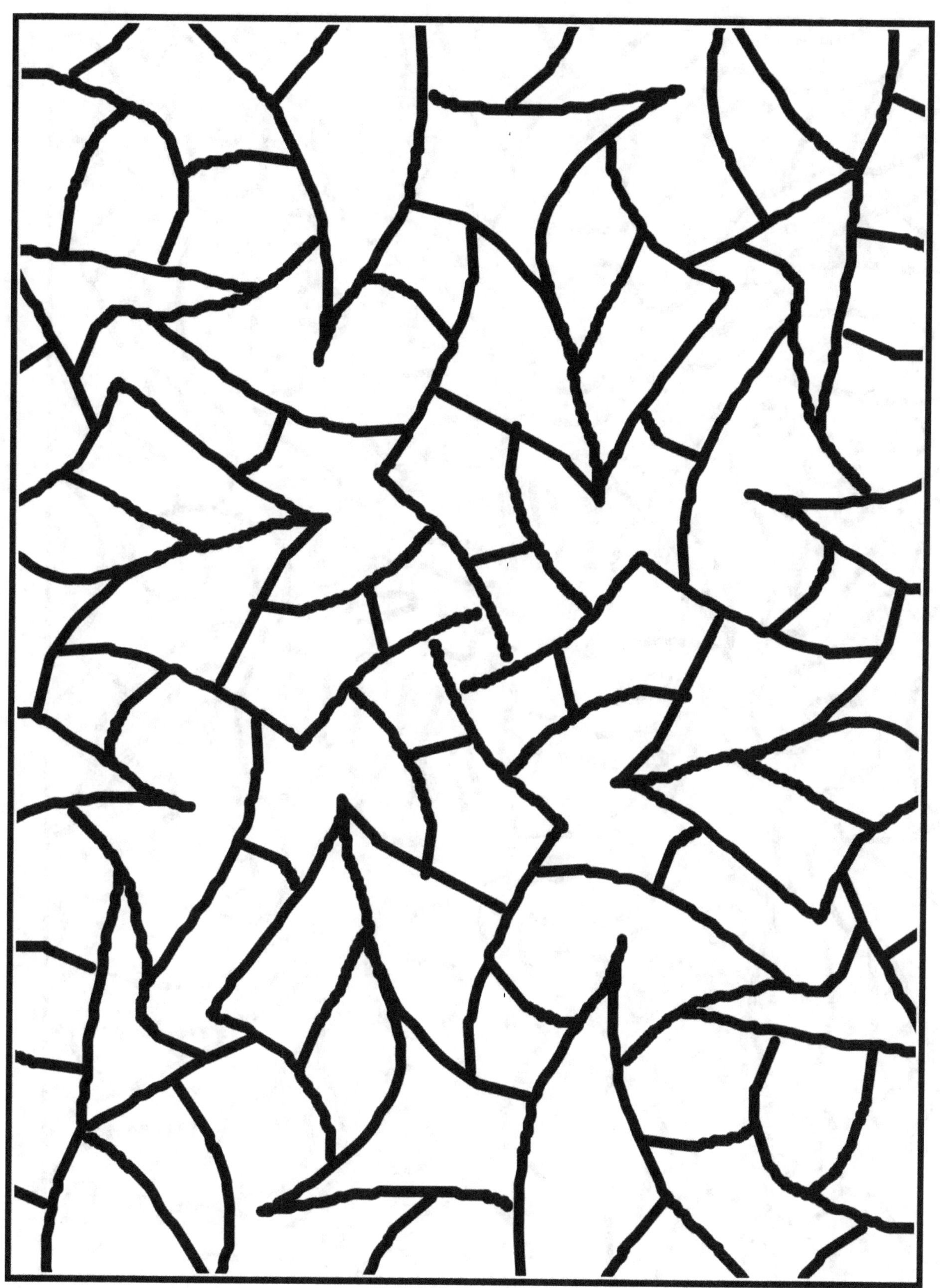

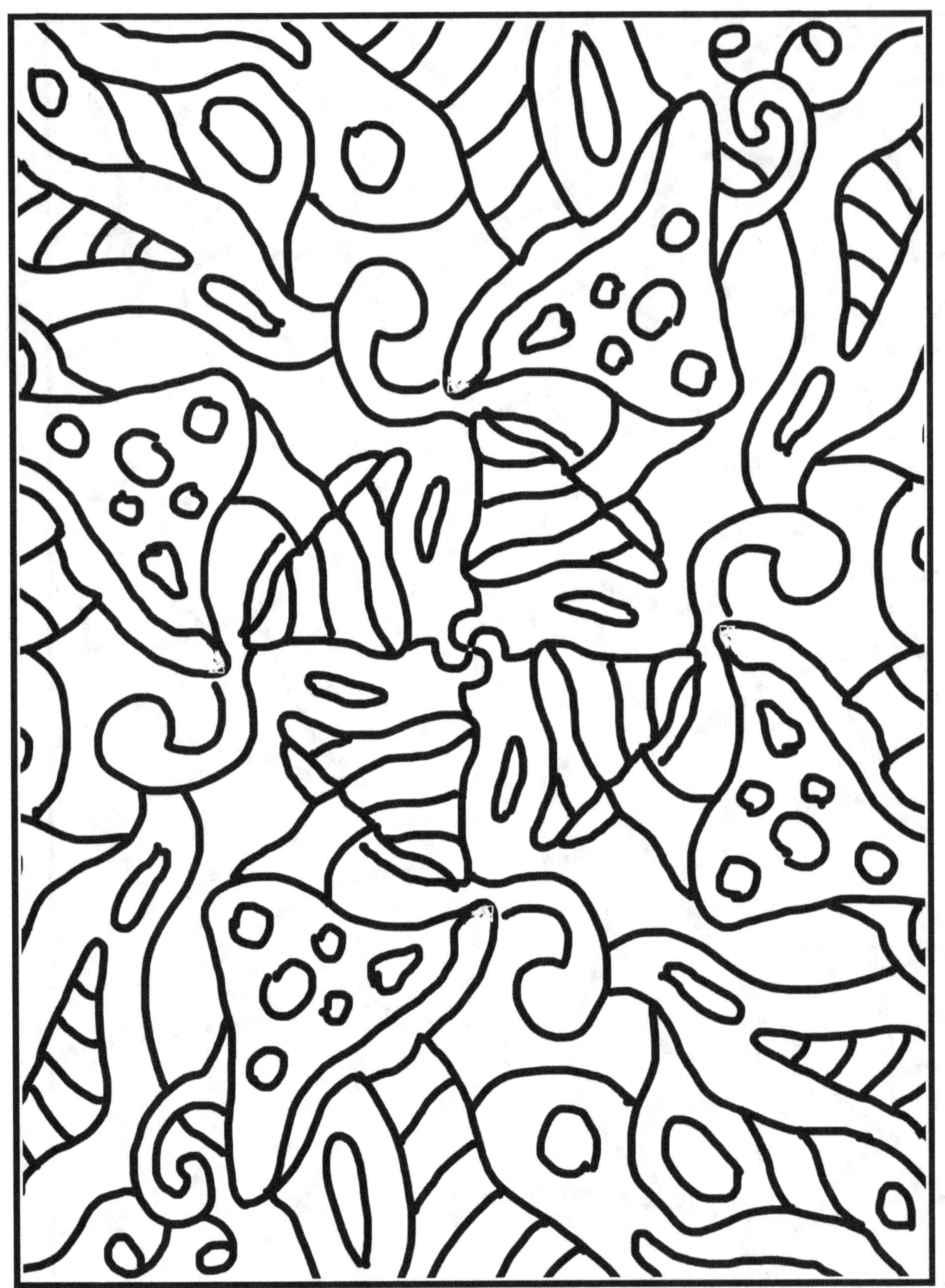

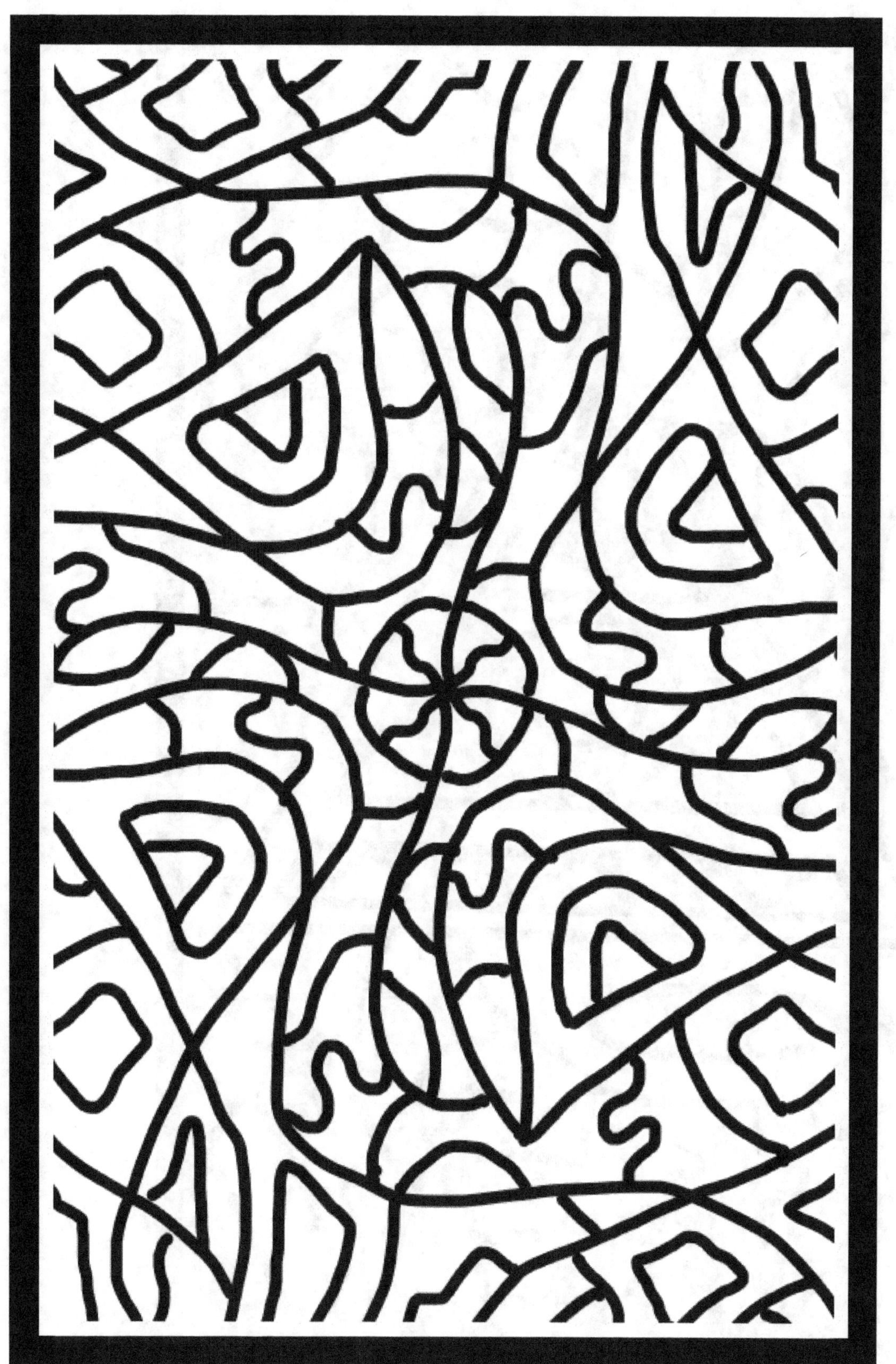

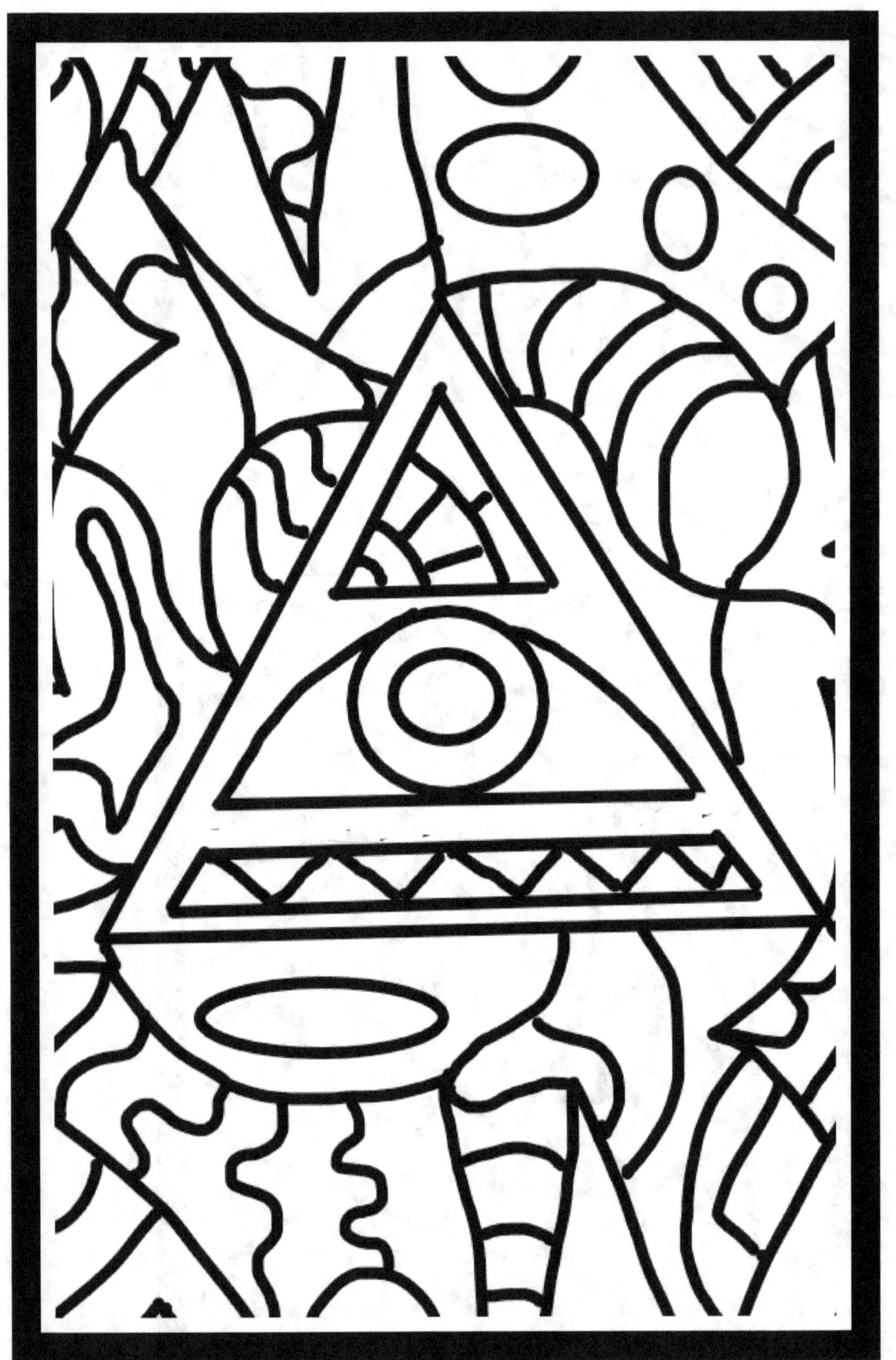

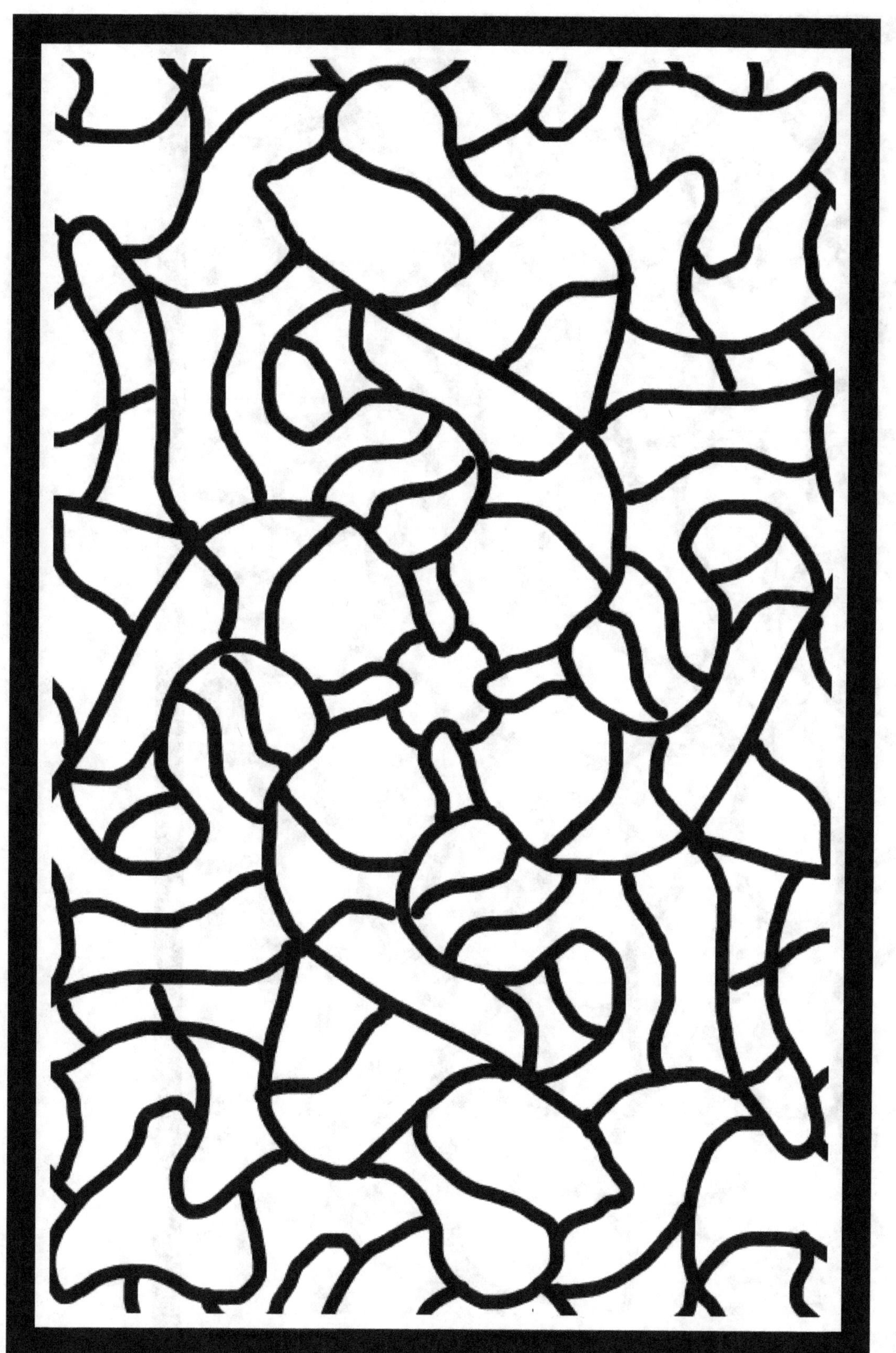

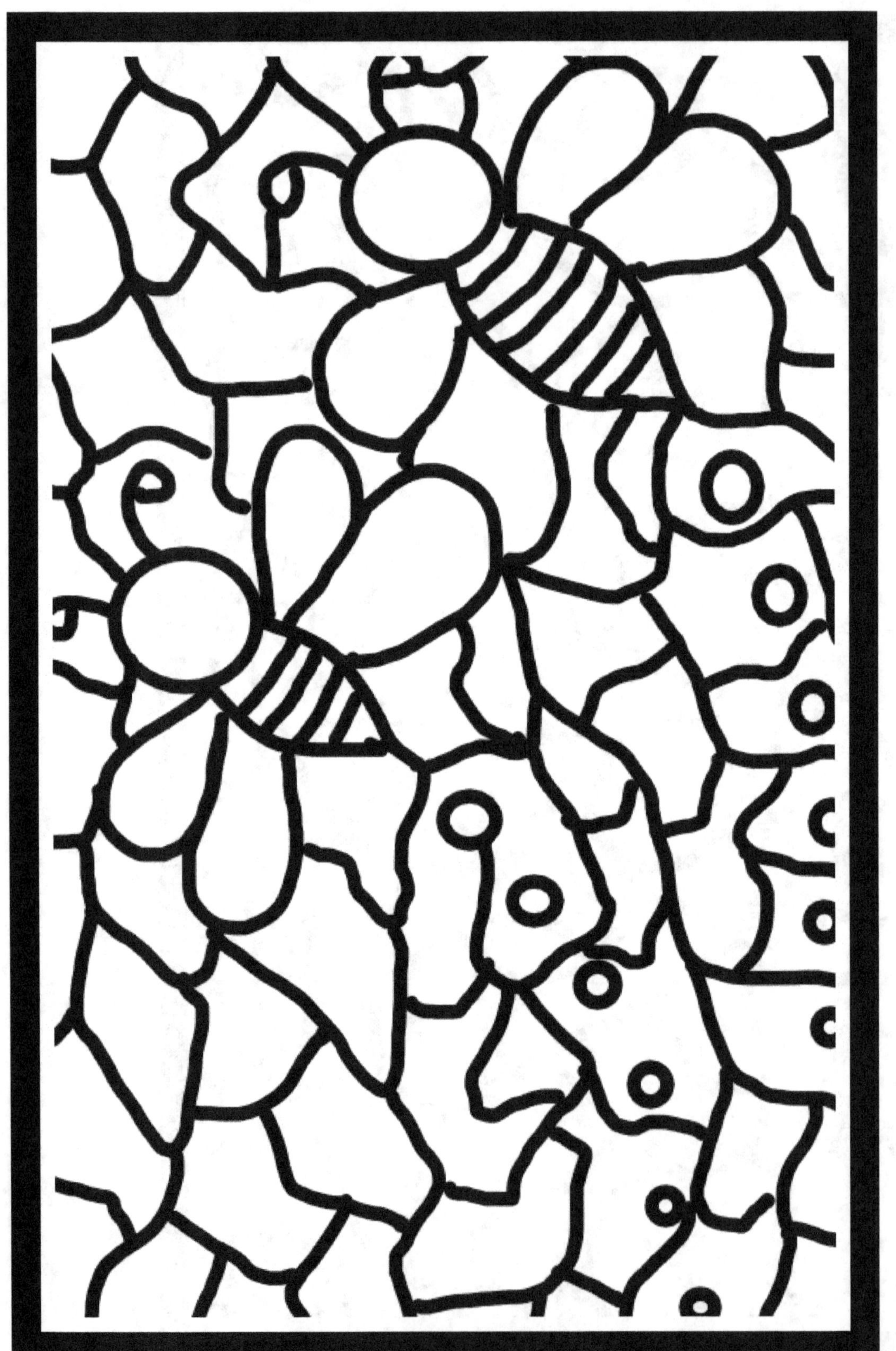

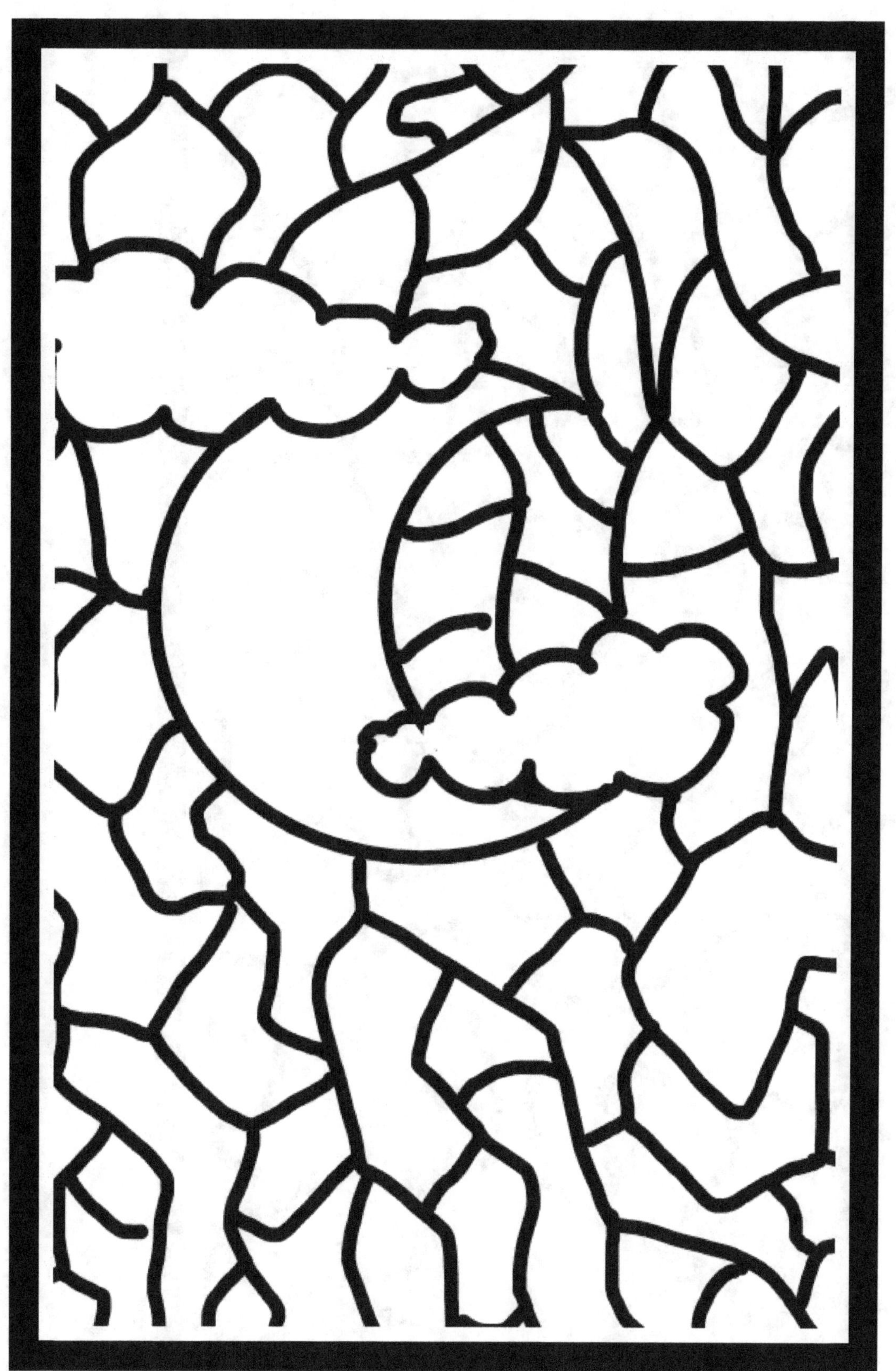

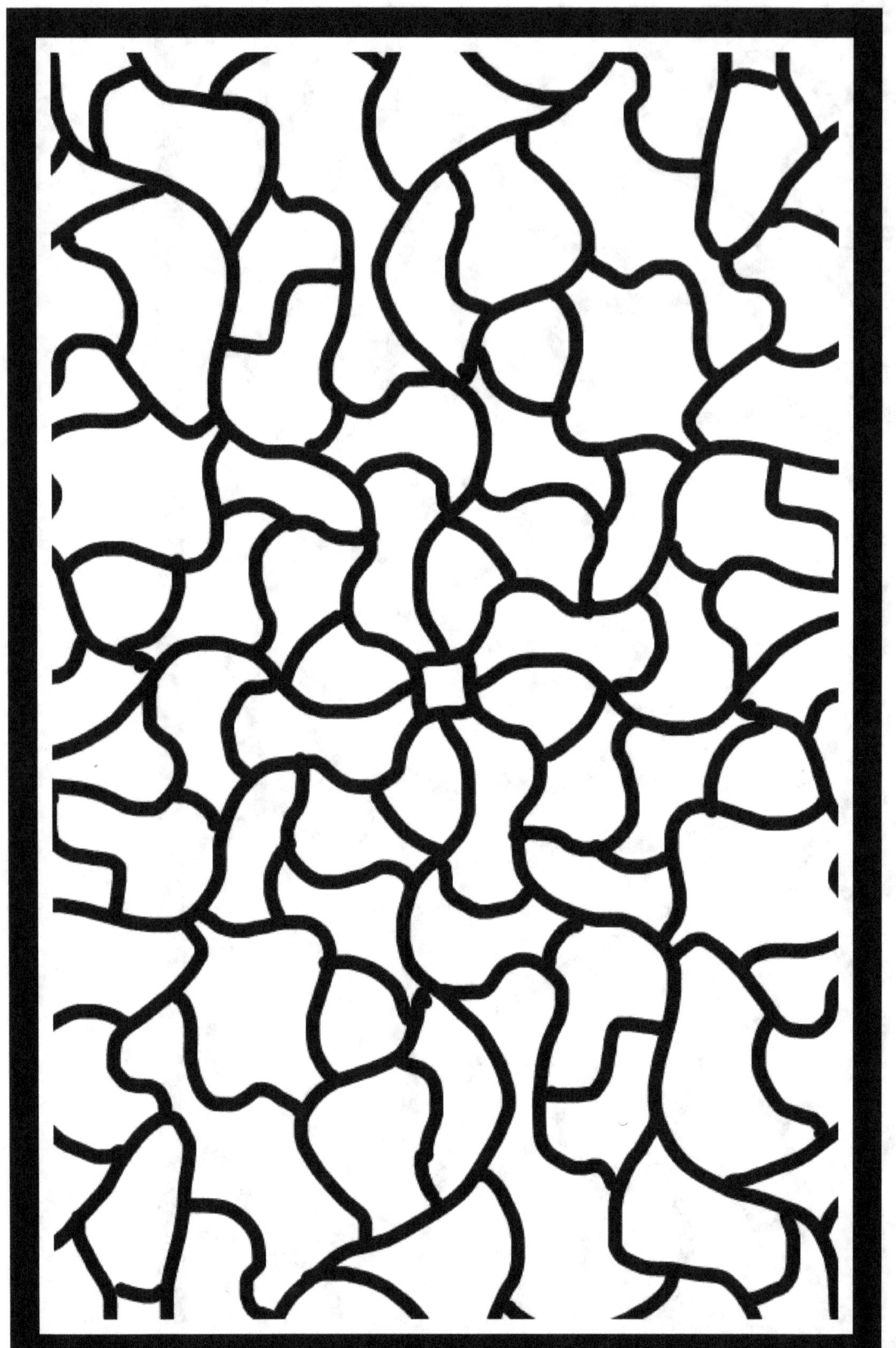

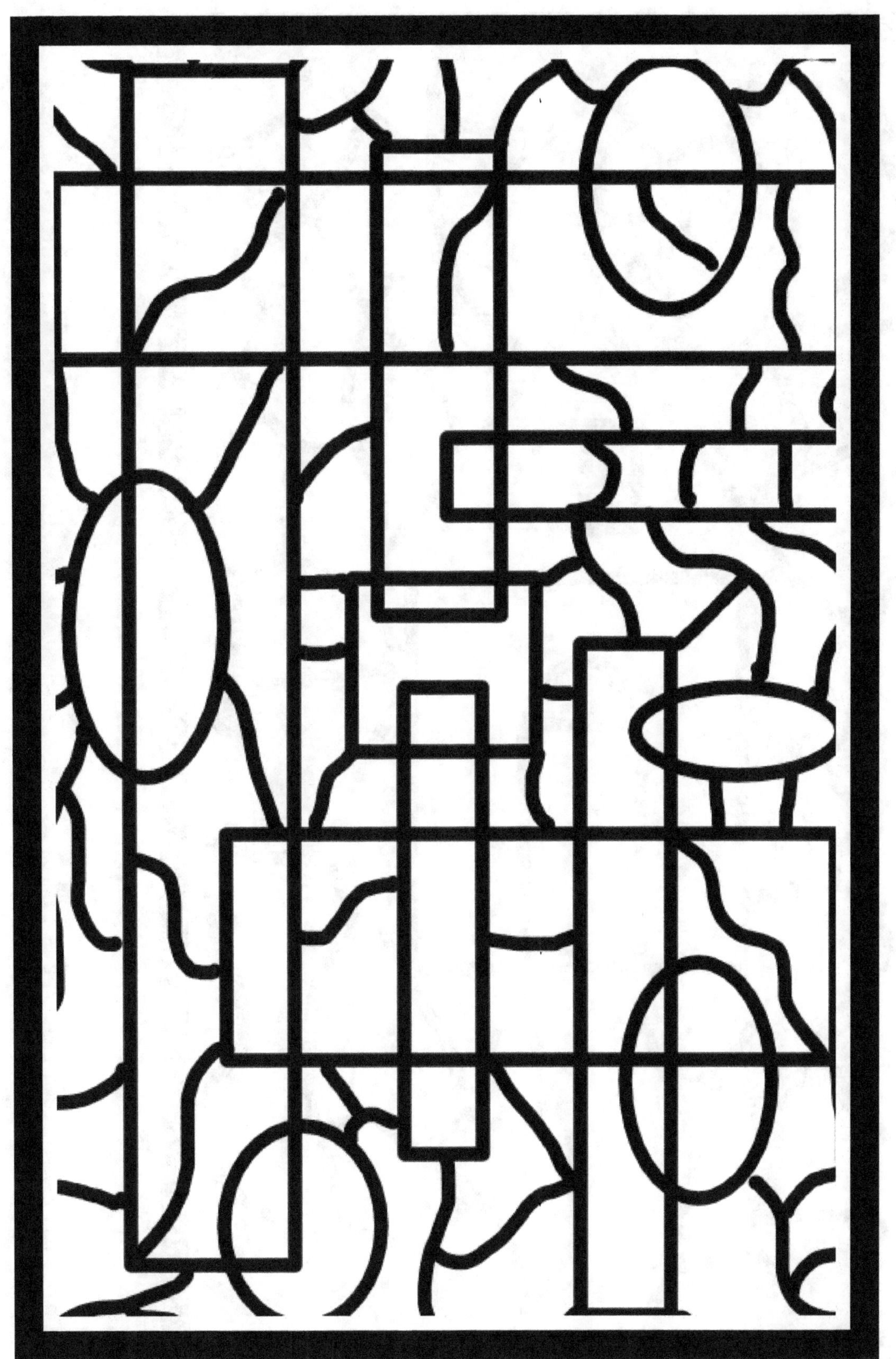

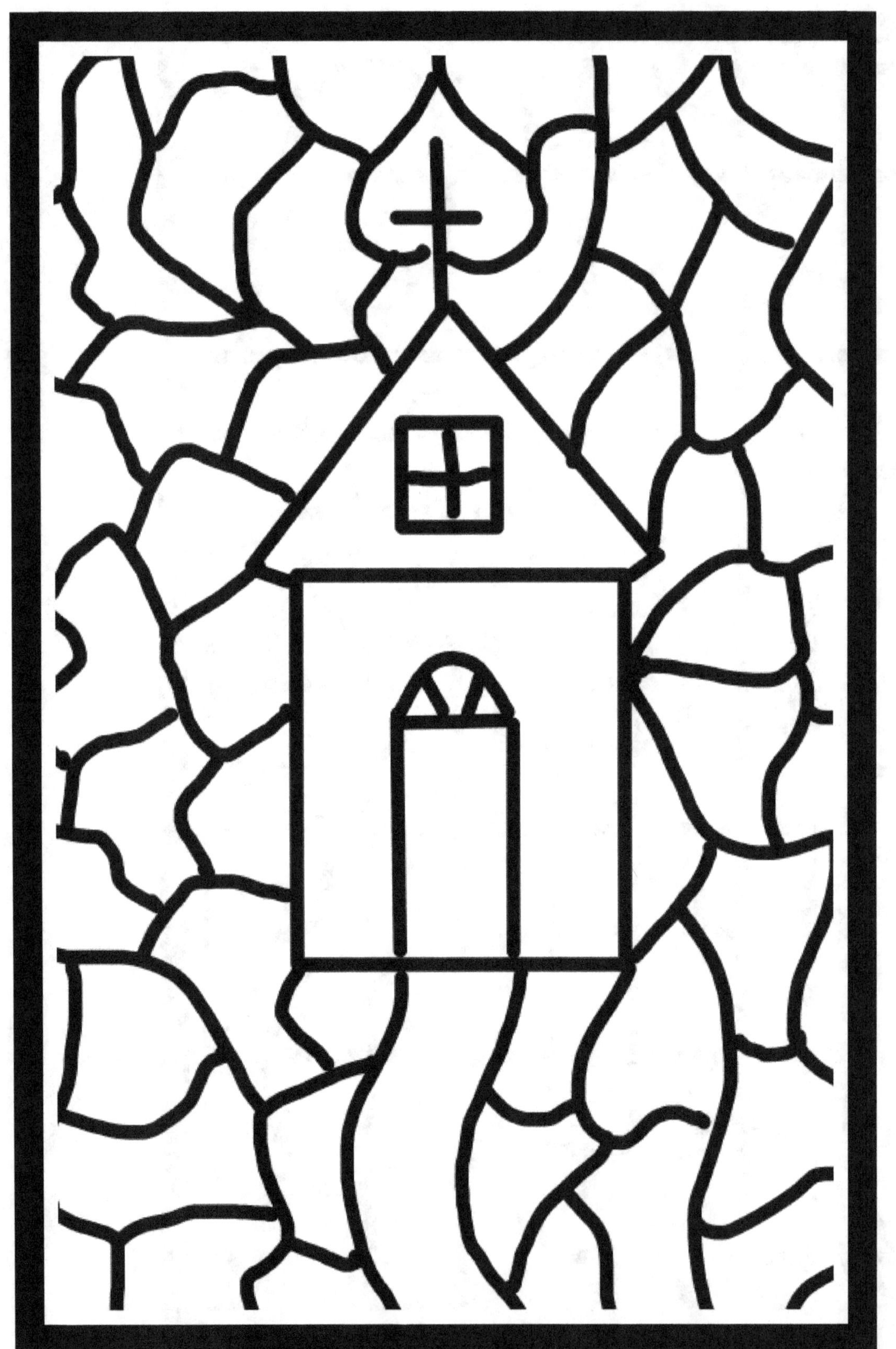

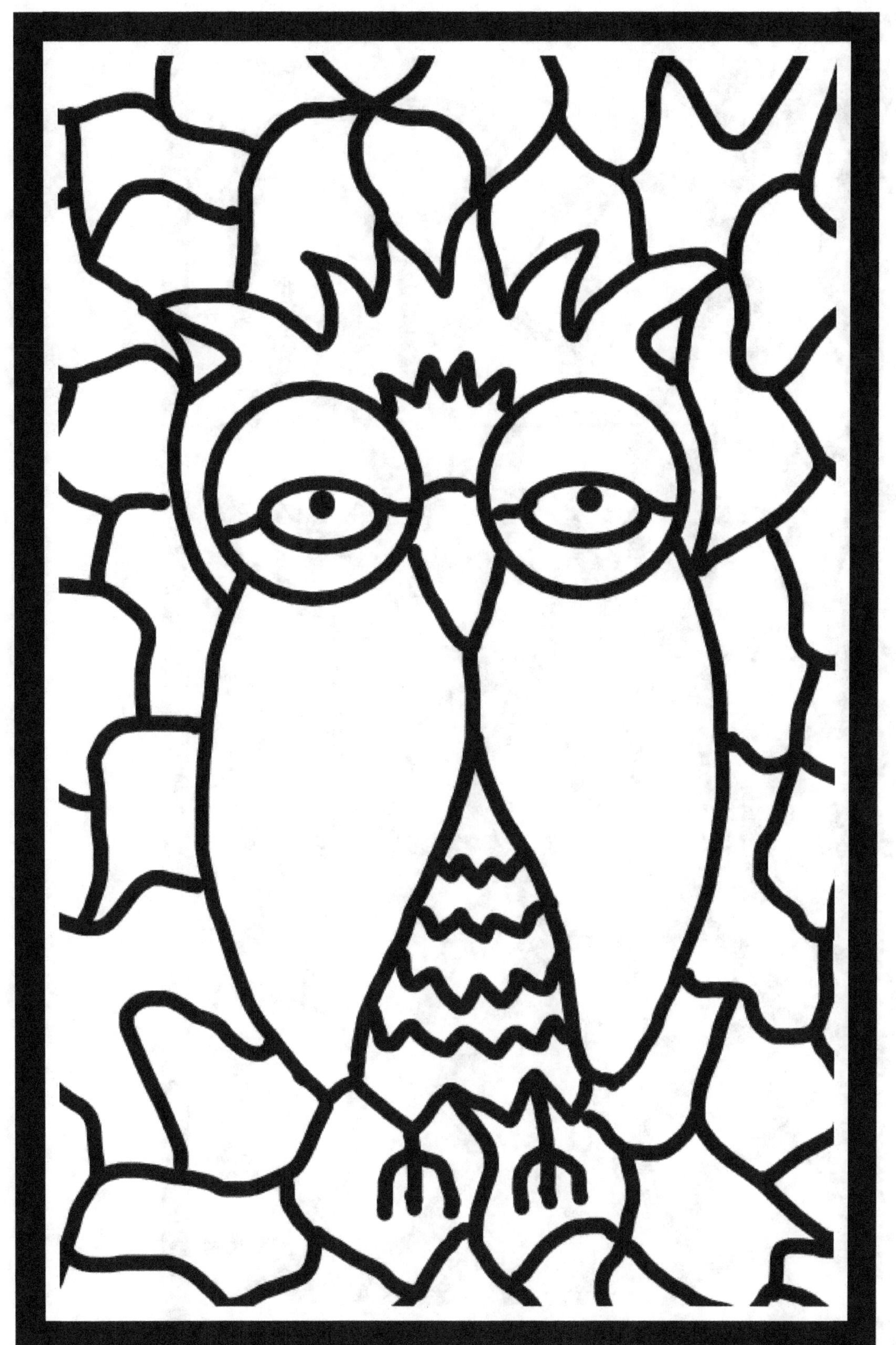

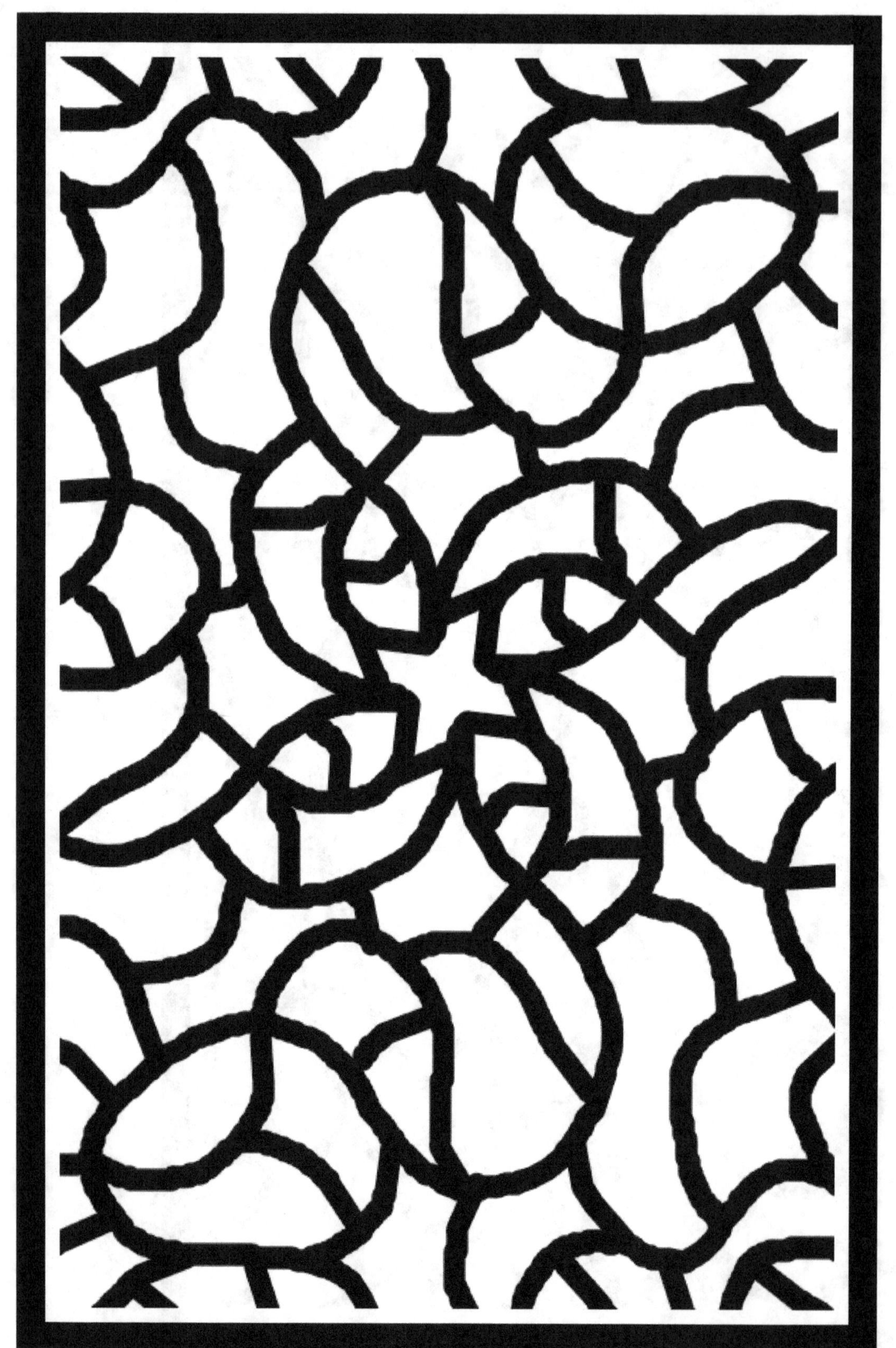

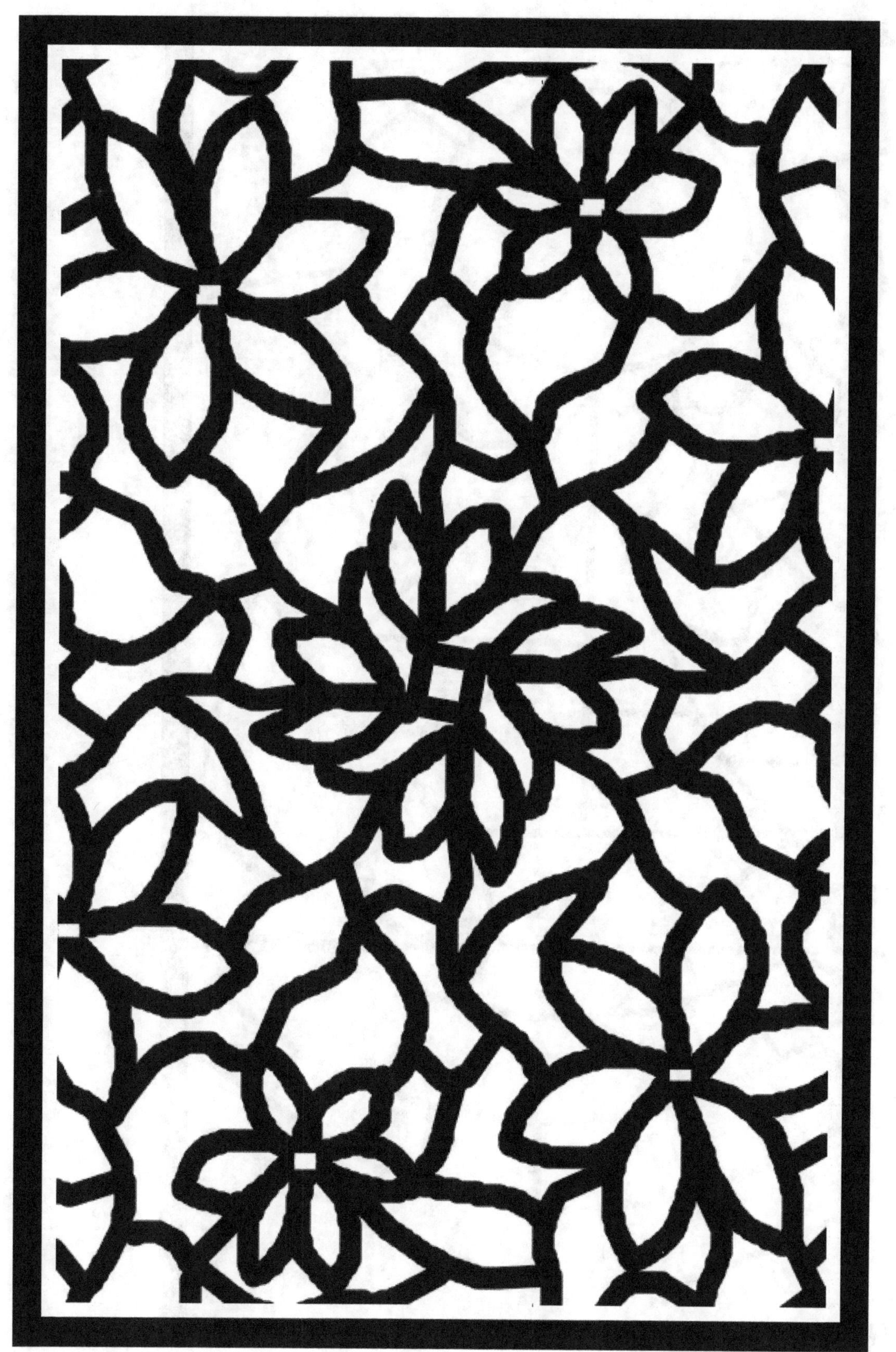

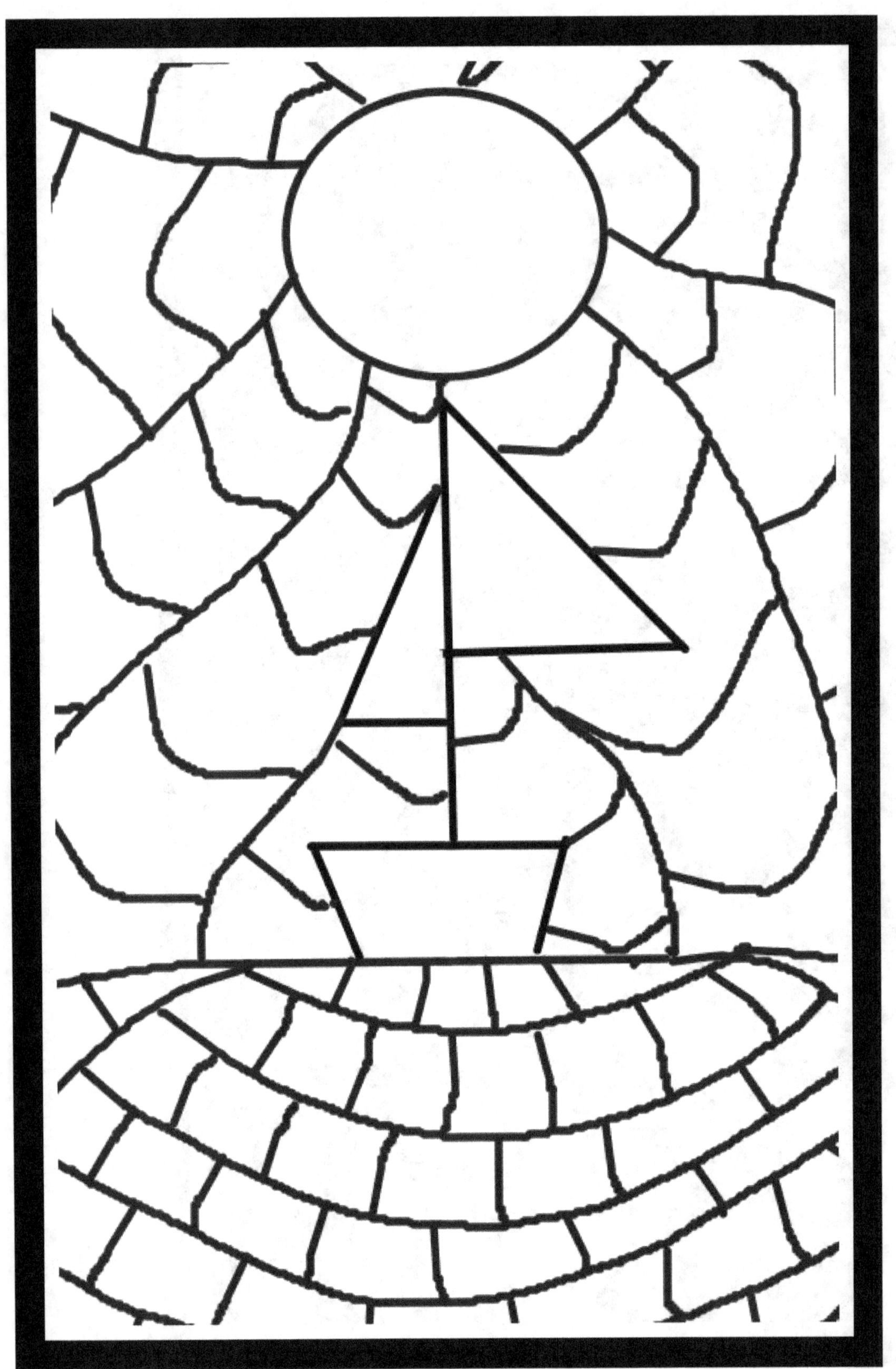

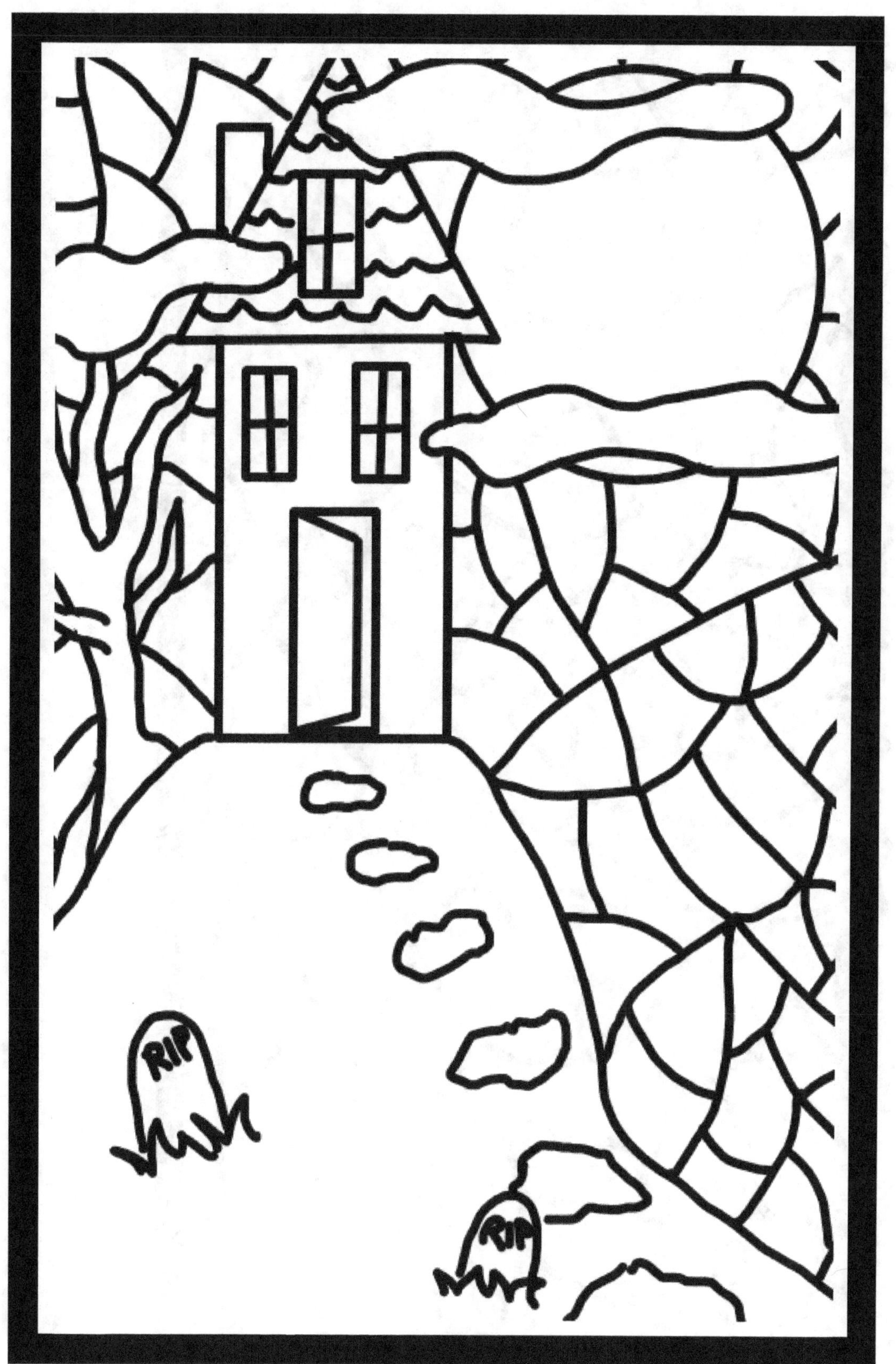

RIP
RIP

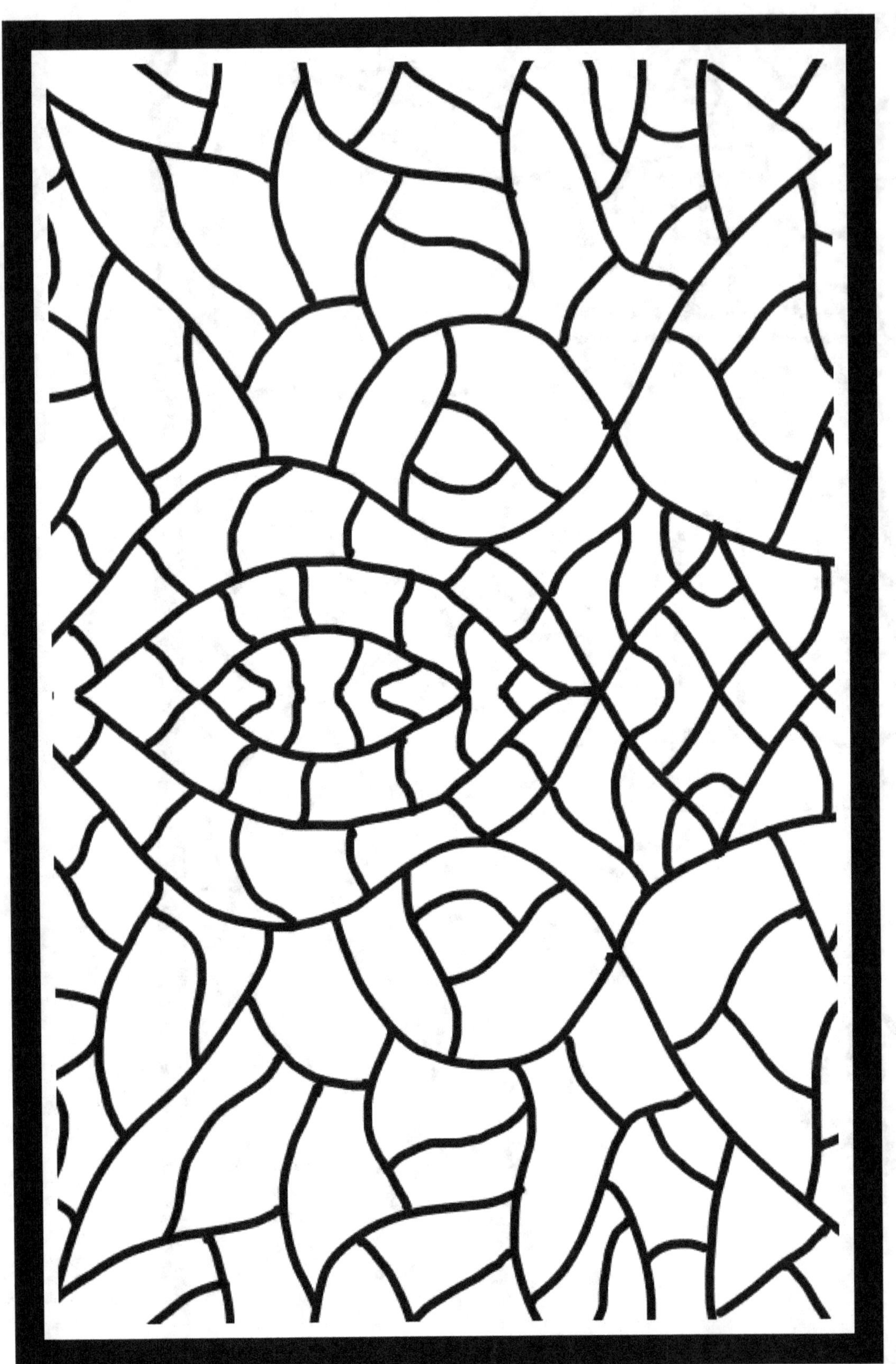

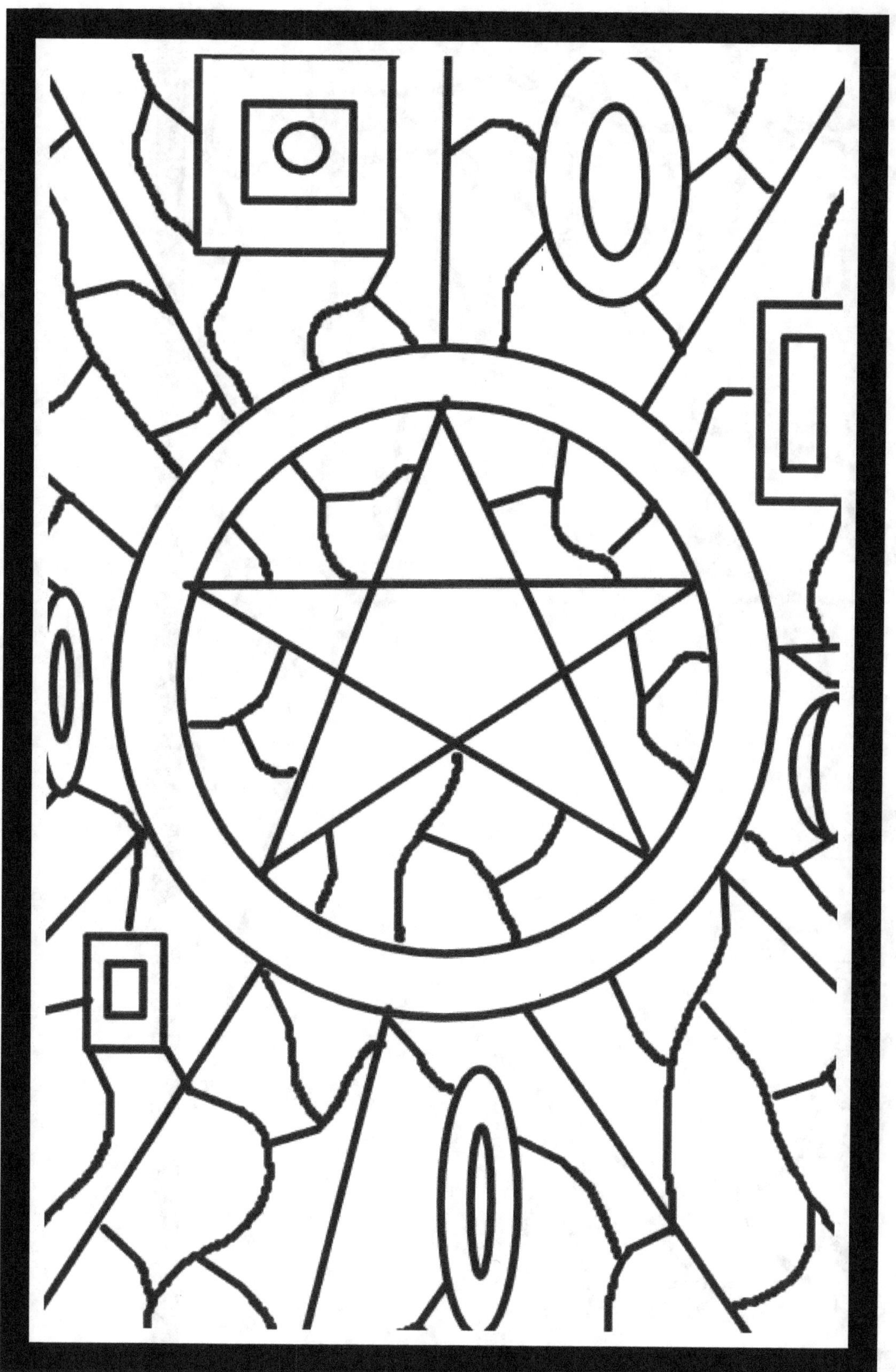

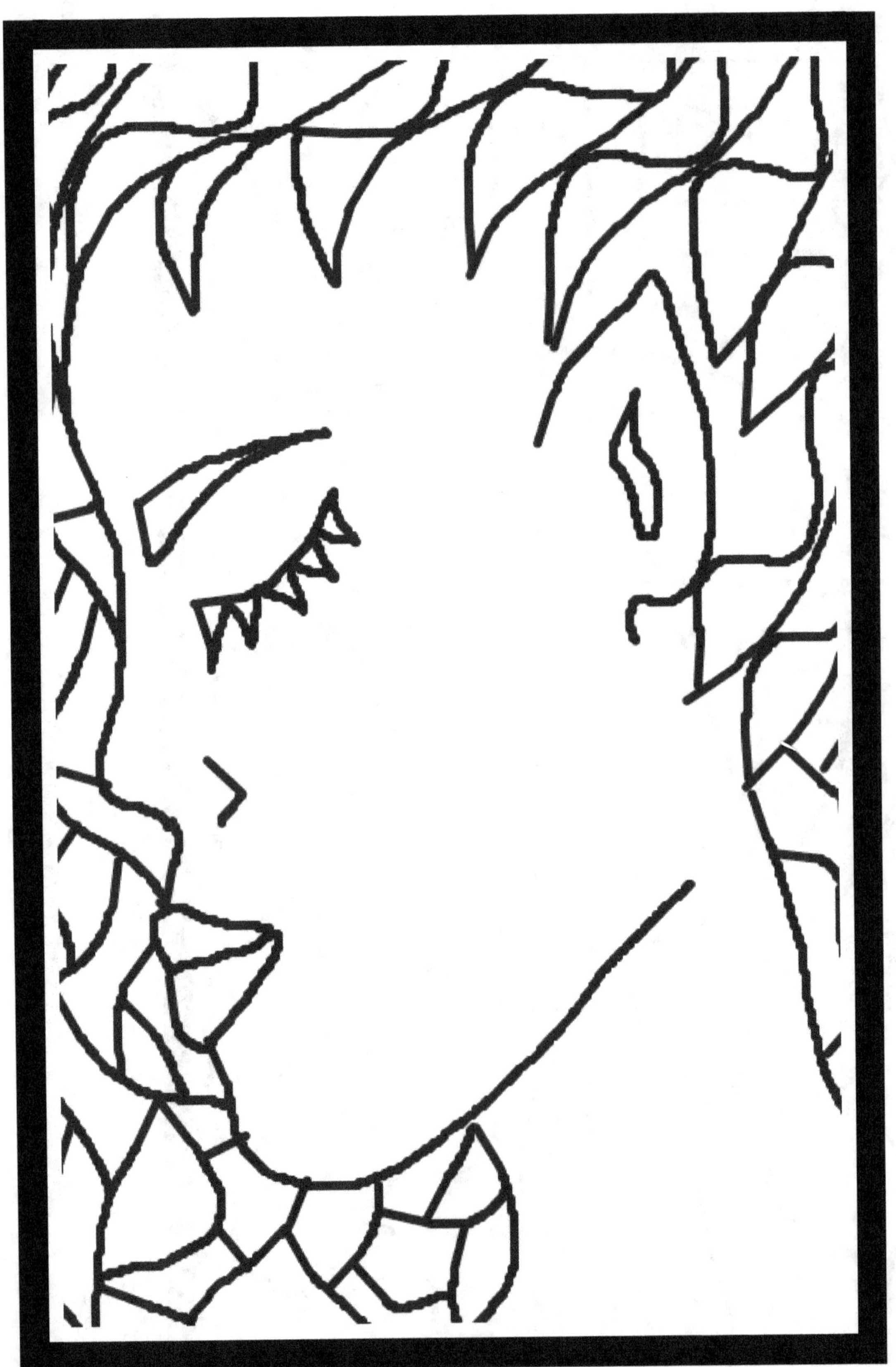

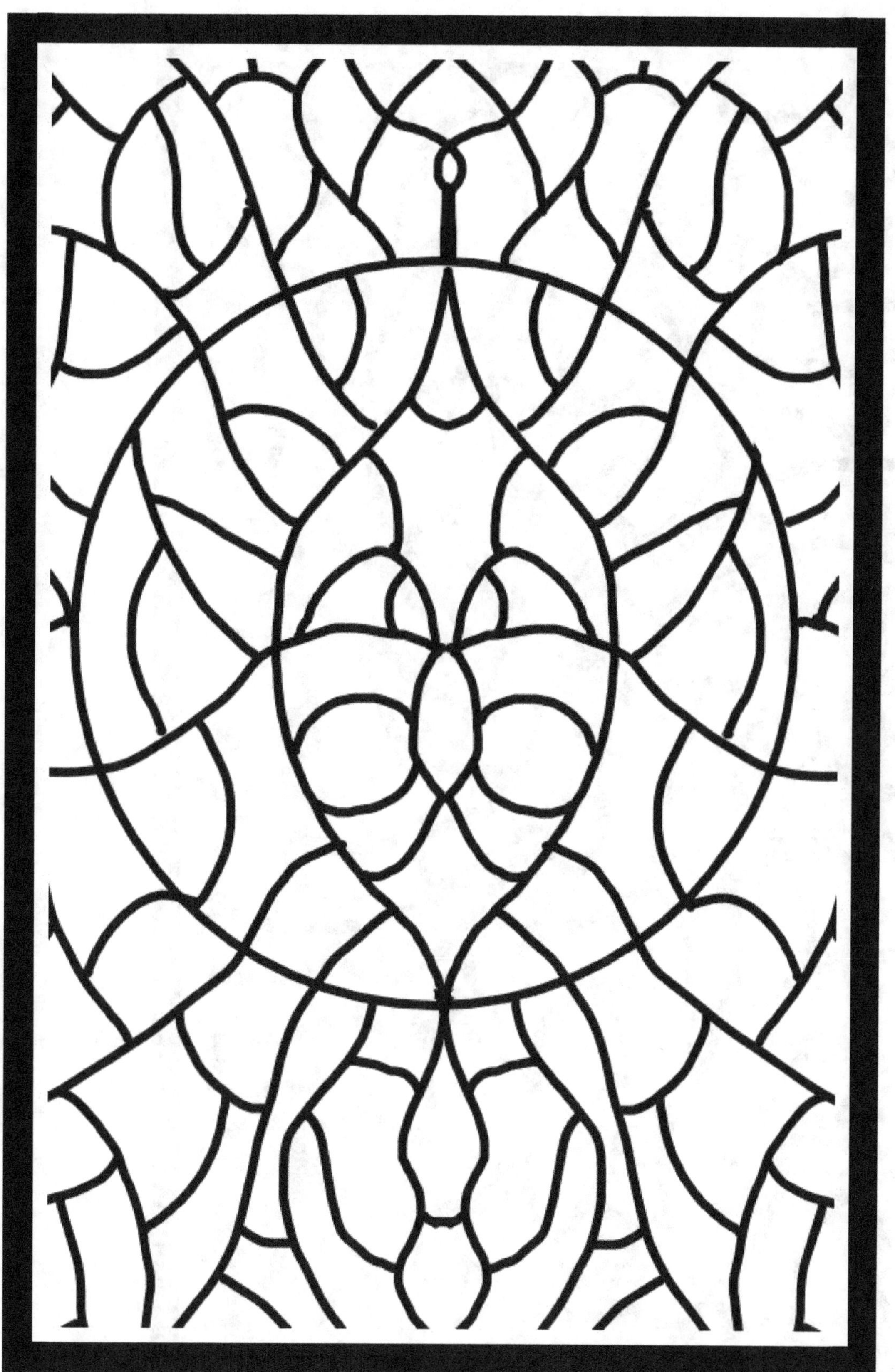

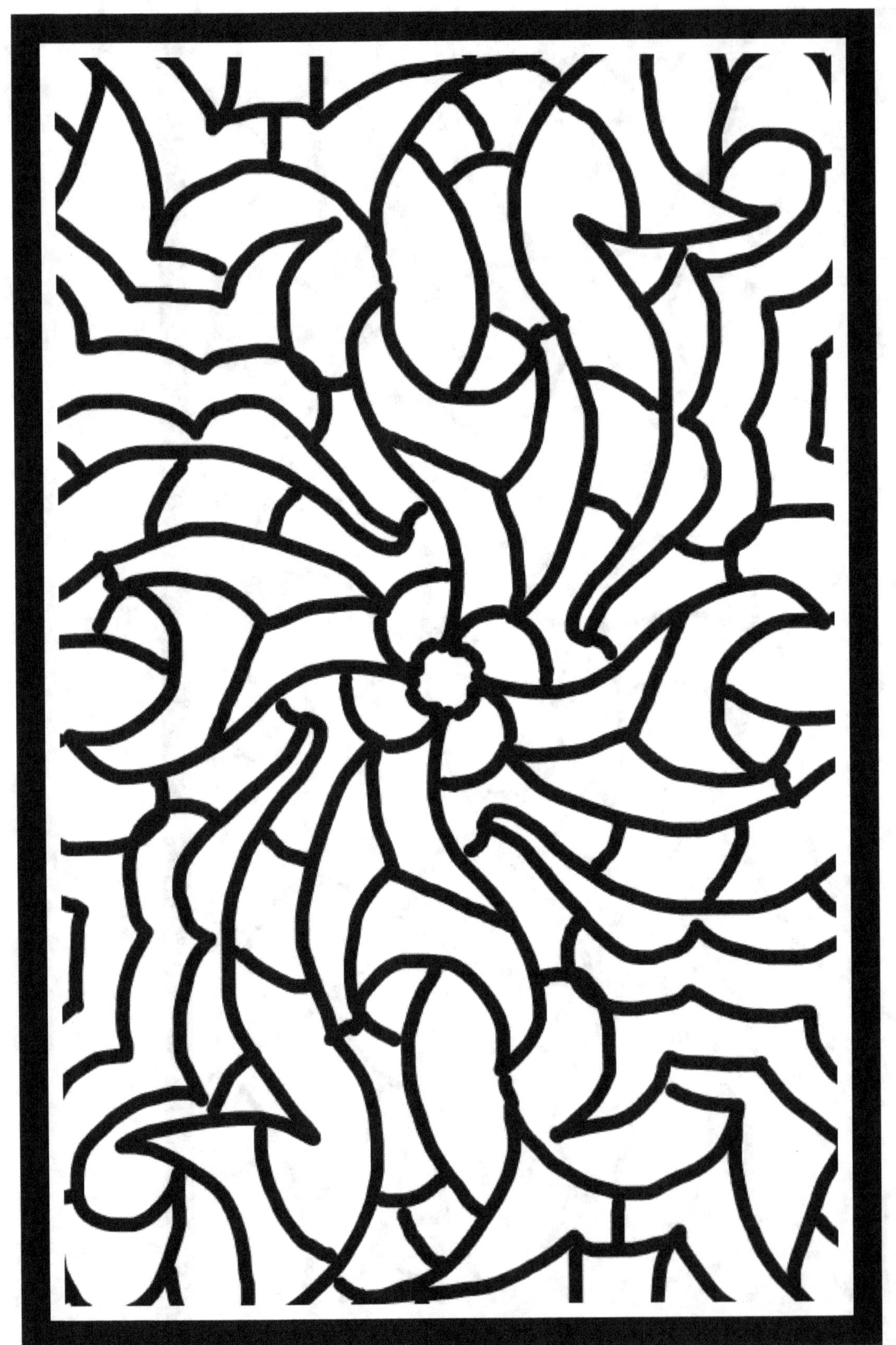

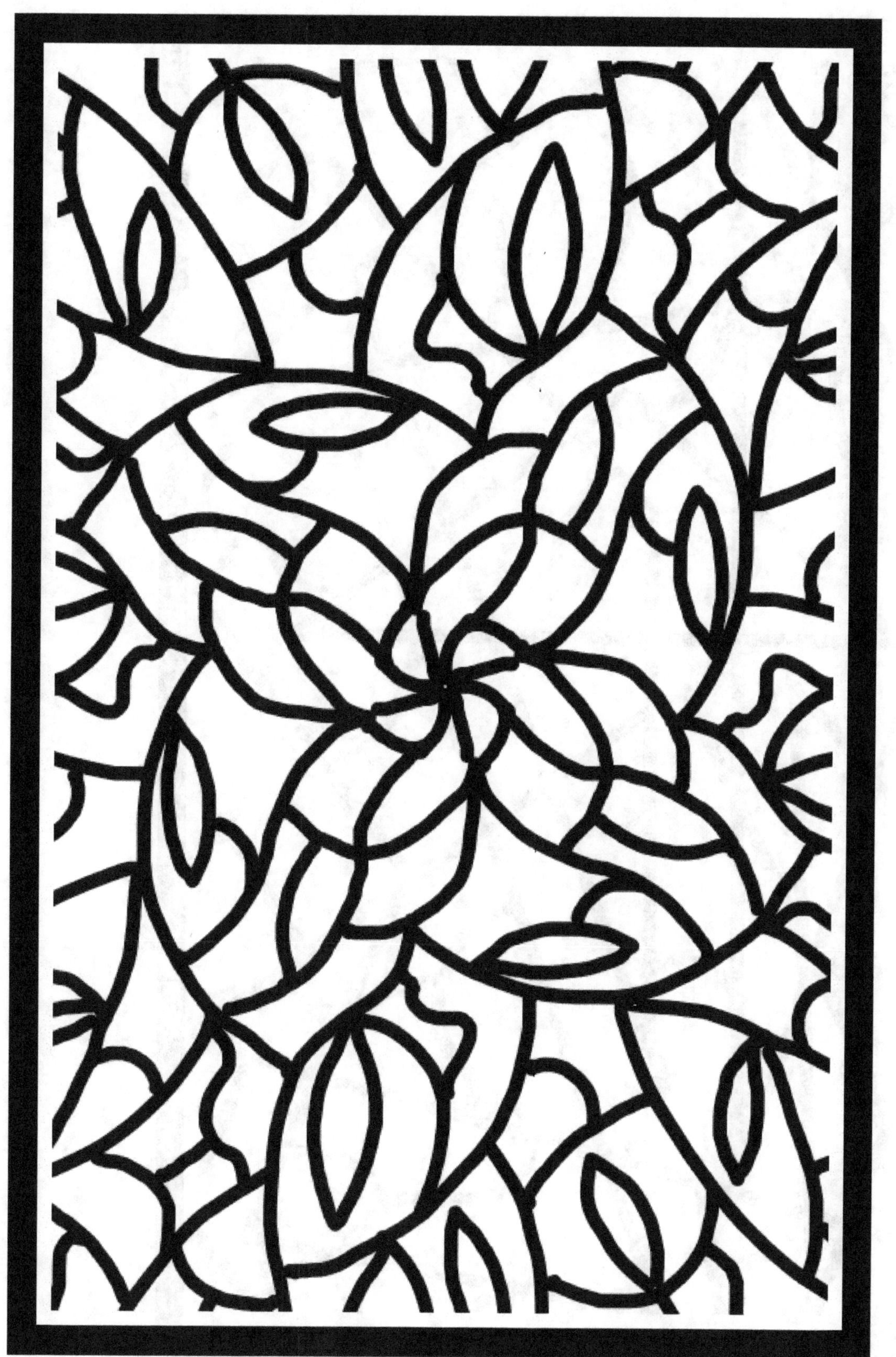

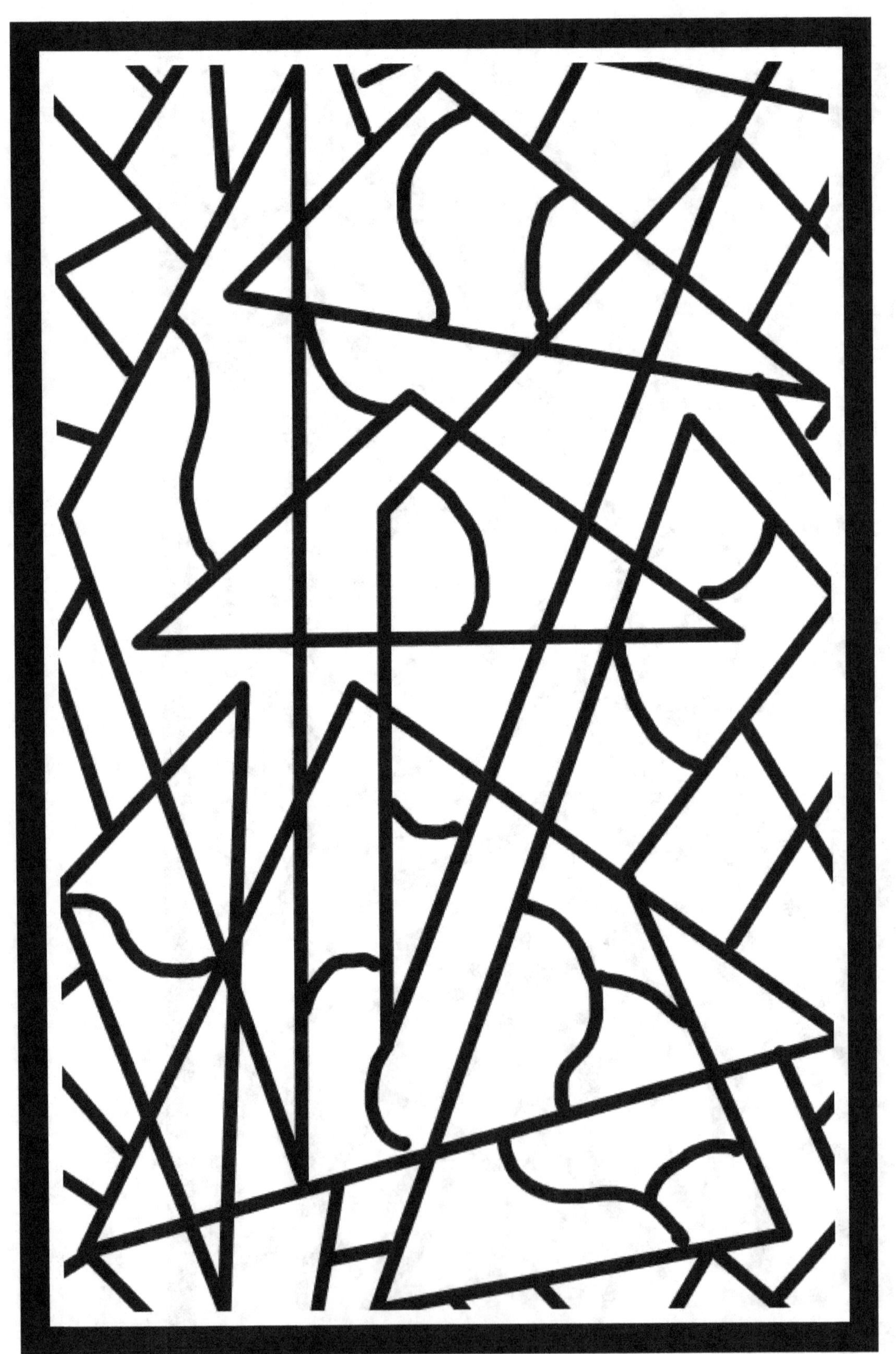

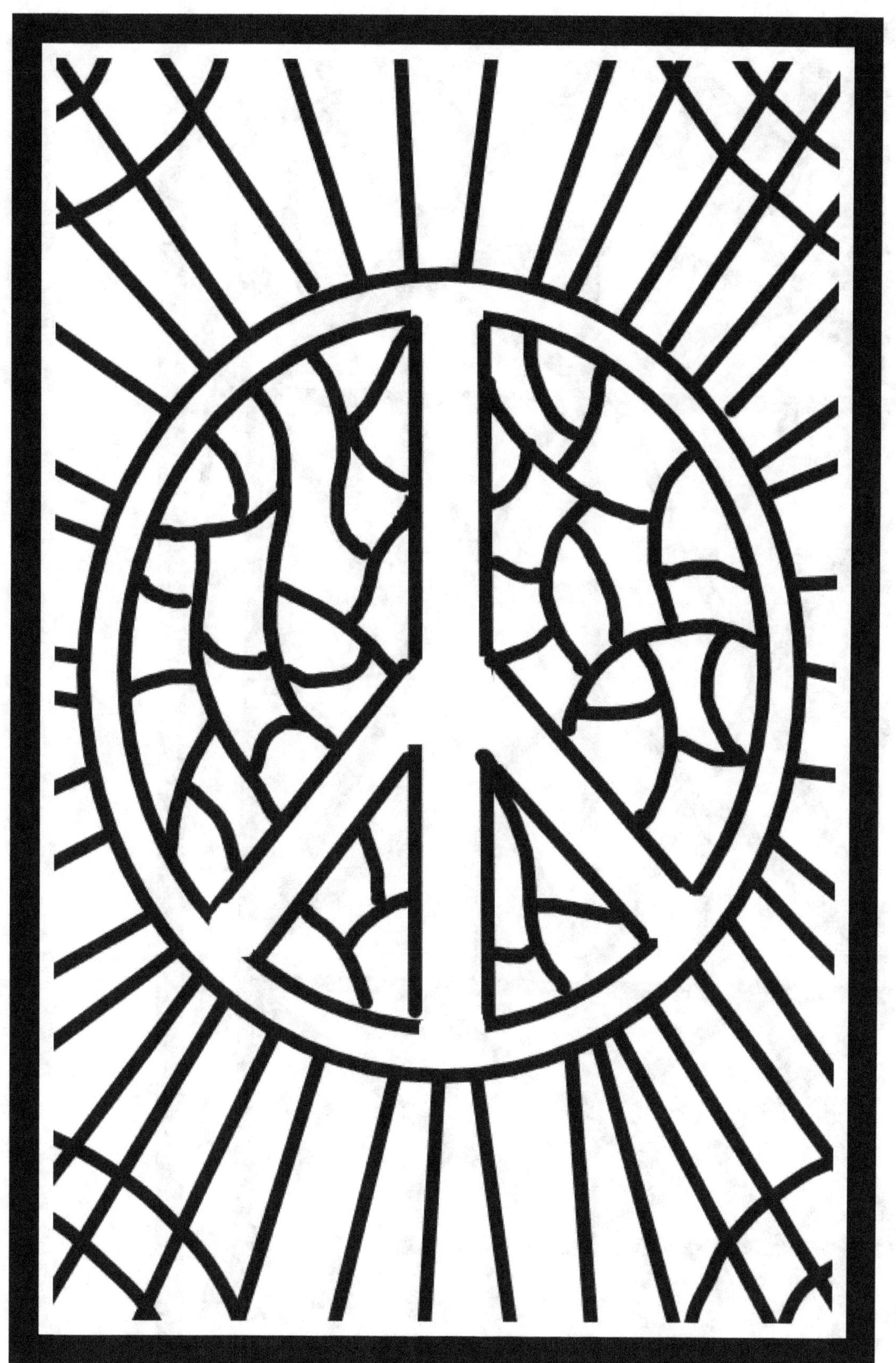

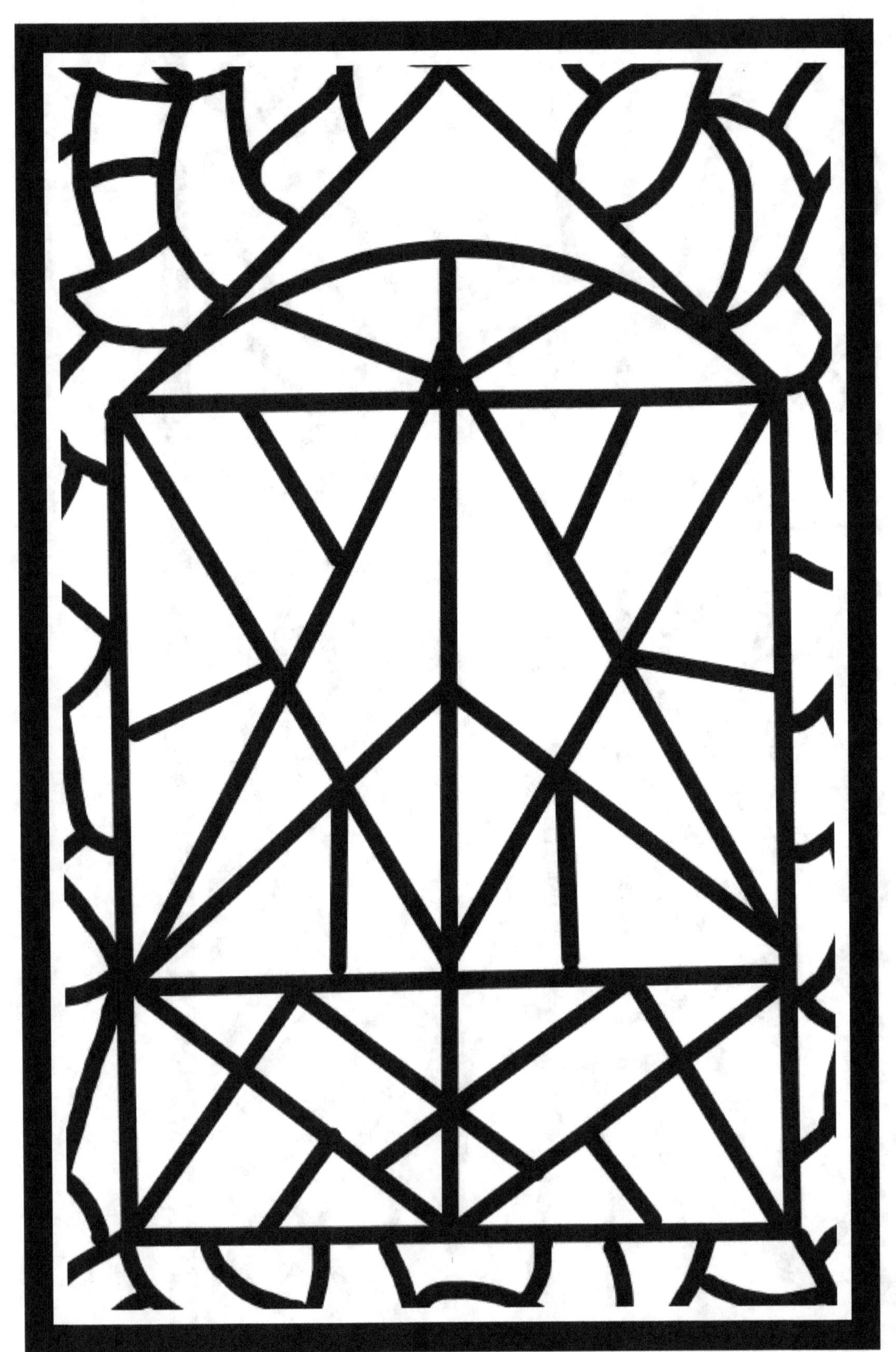

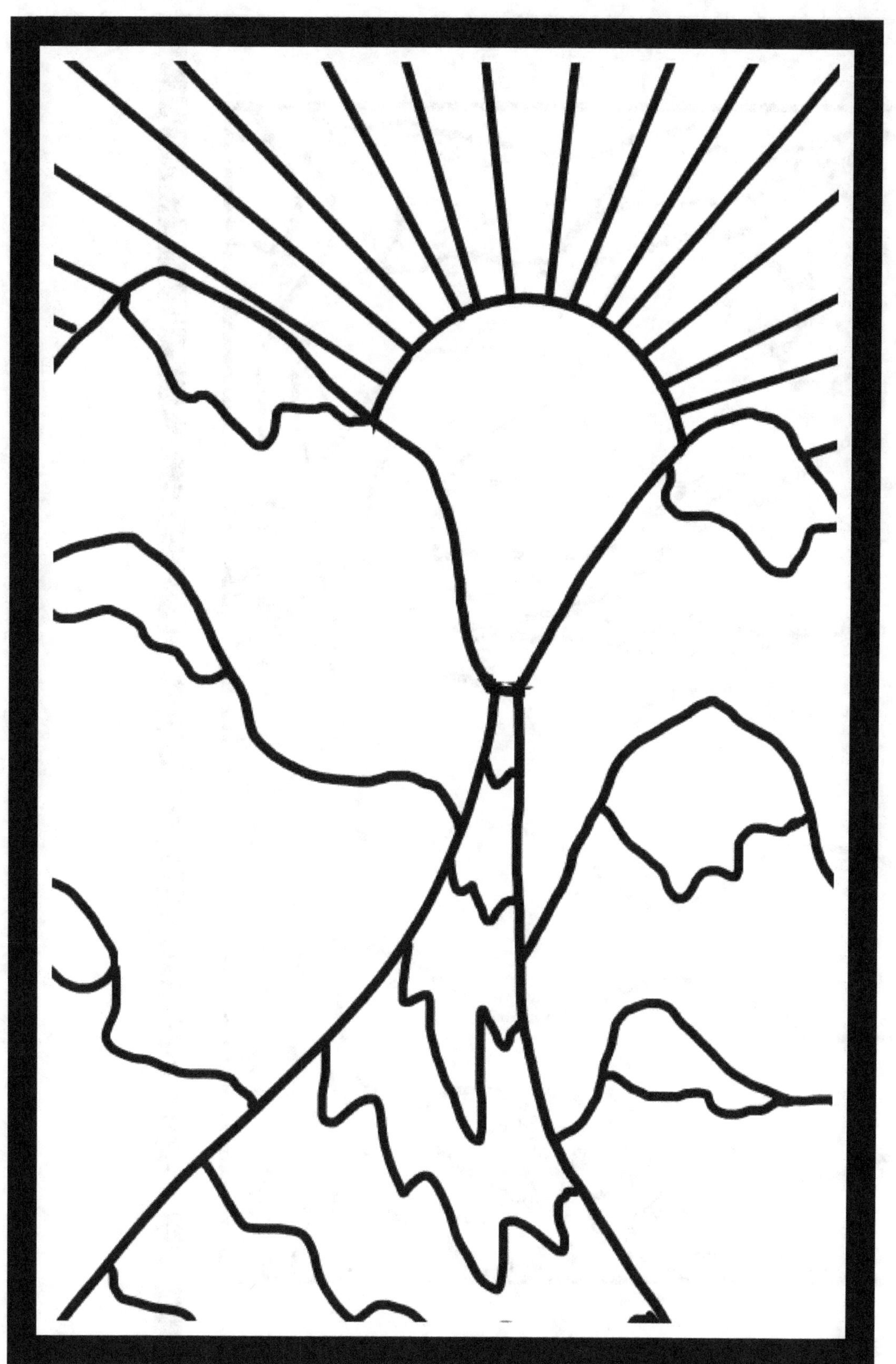

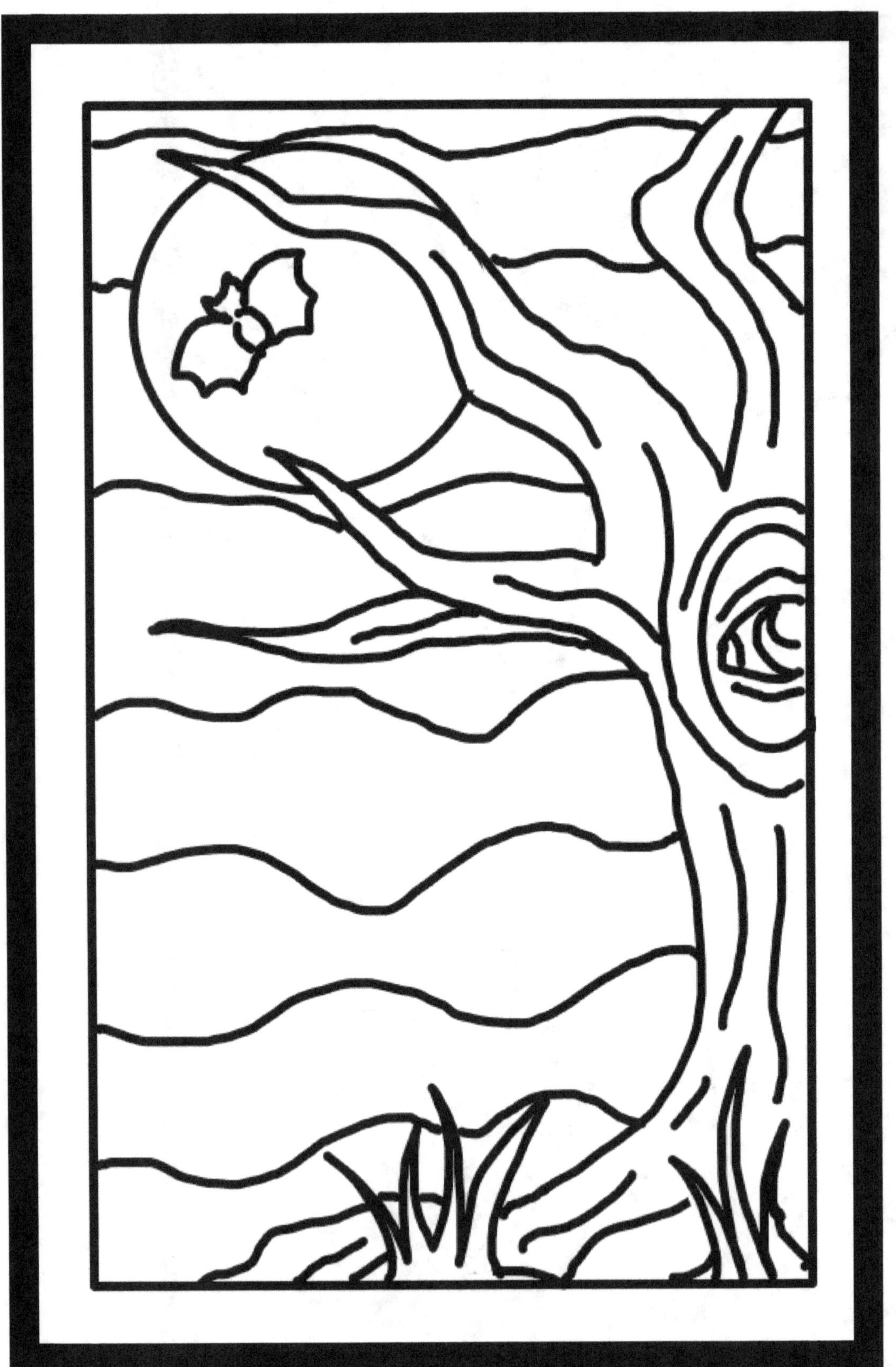

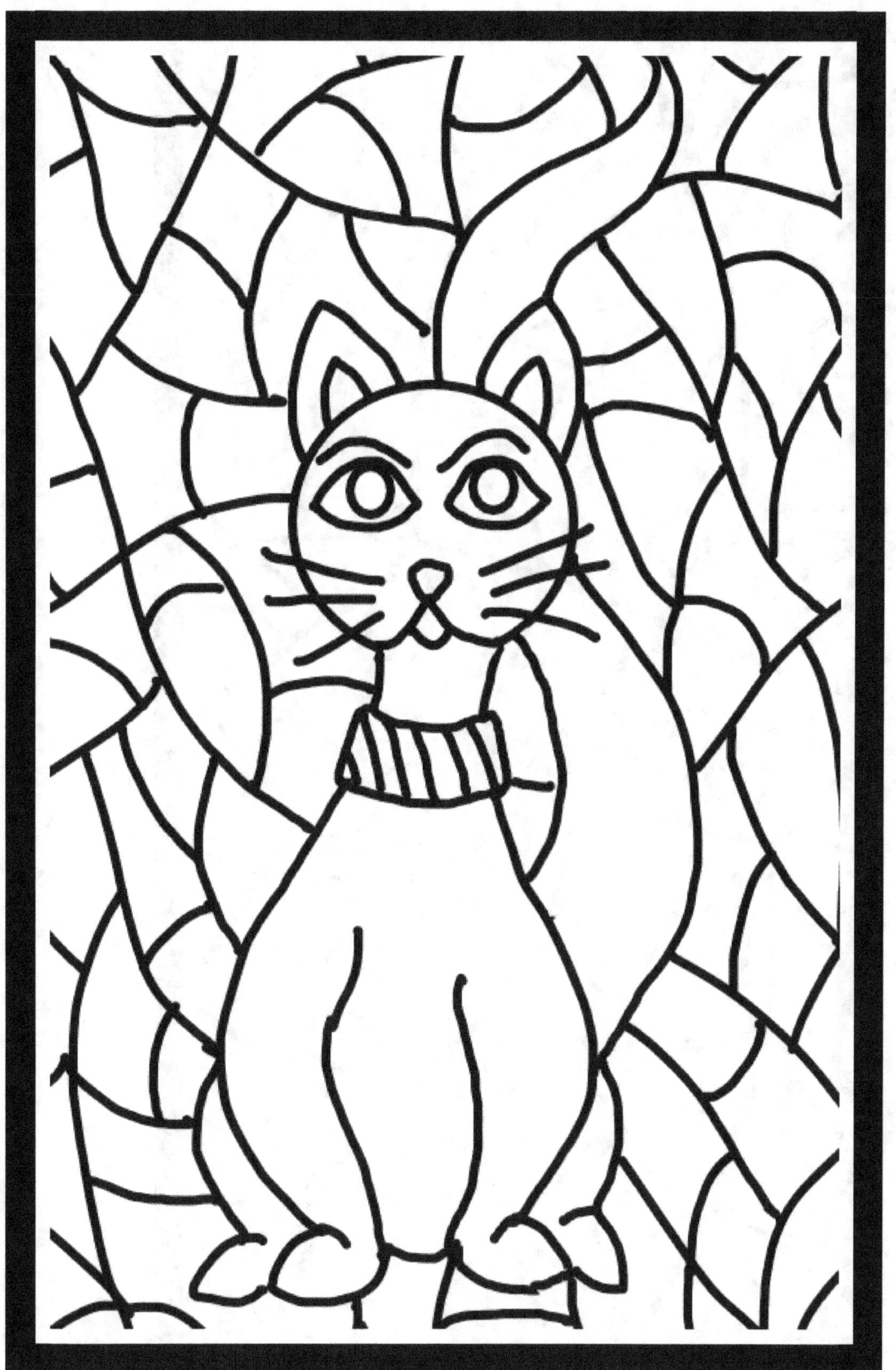

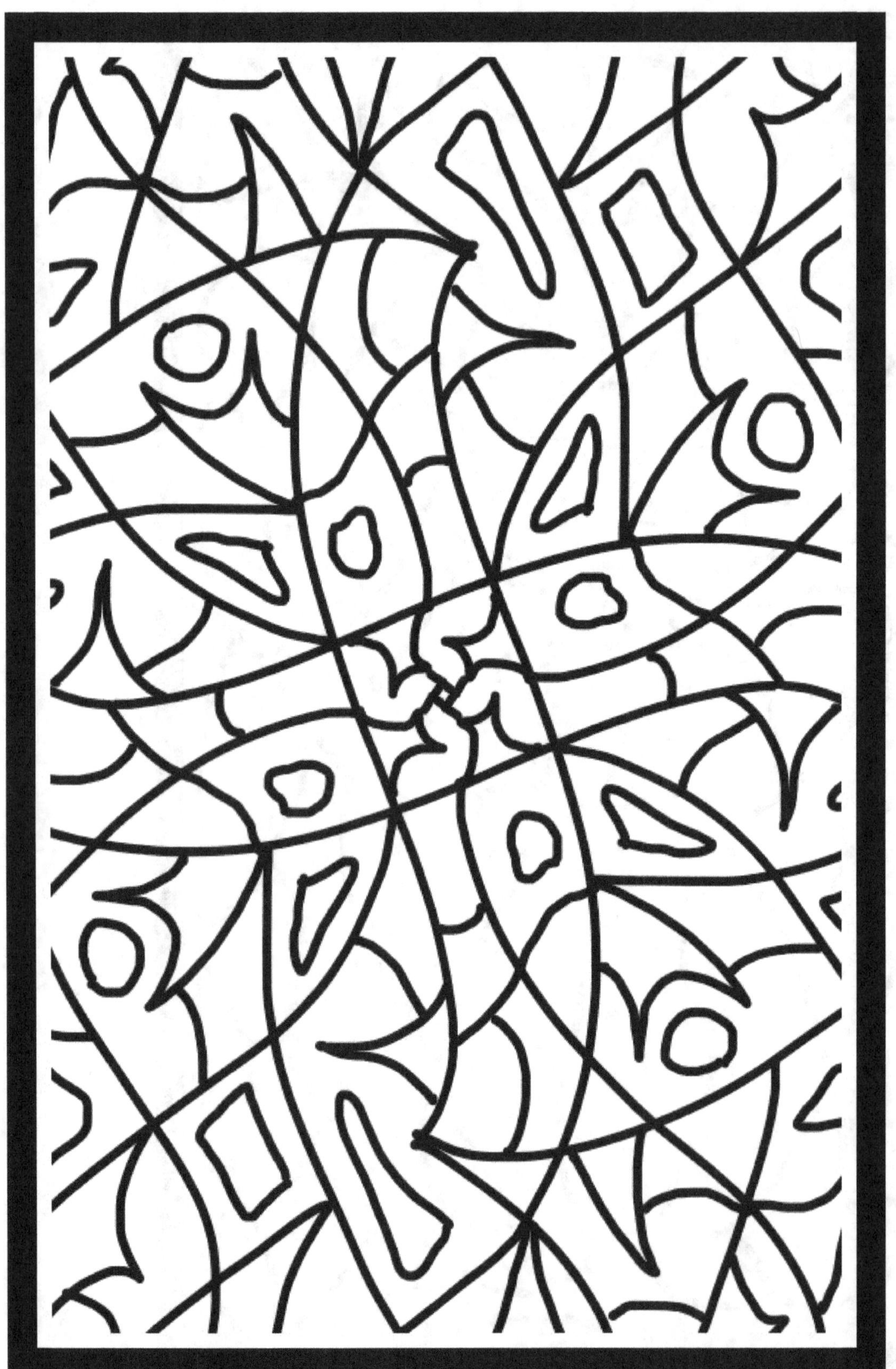

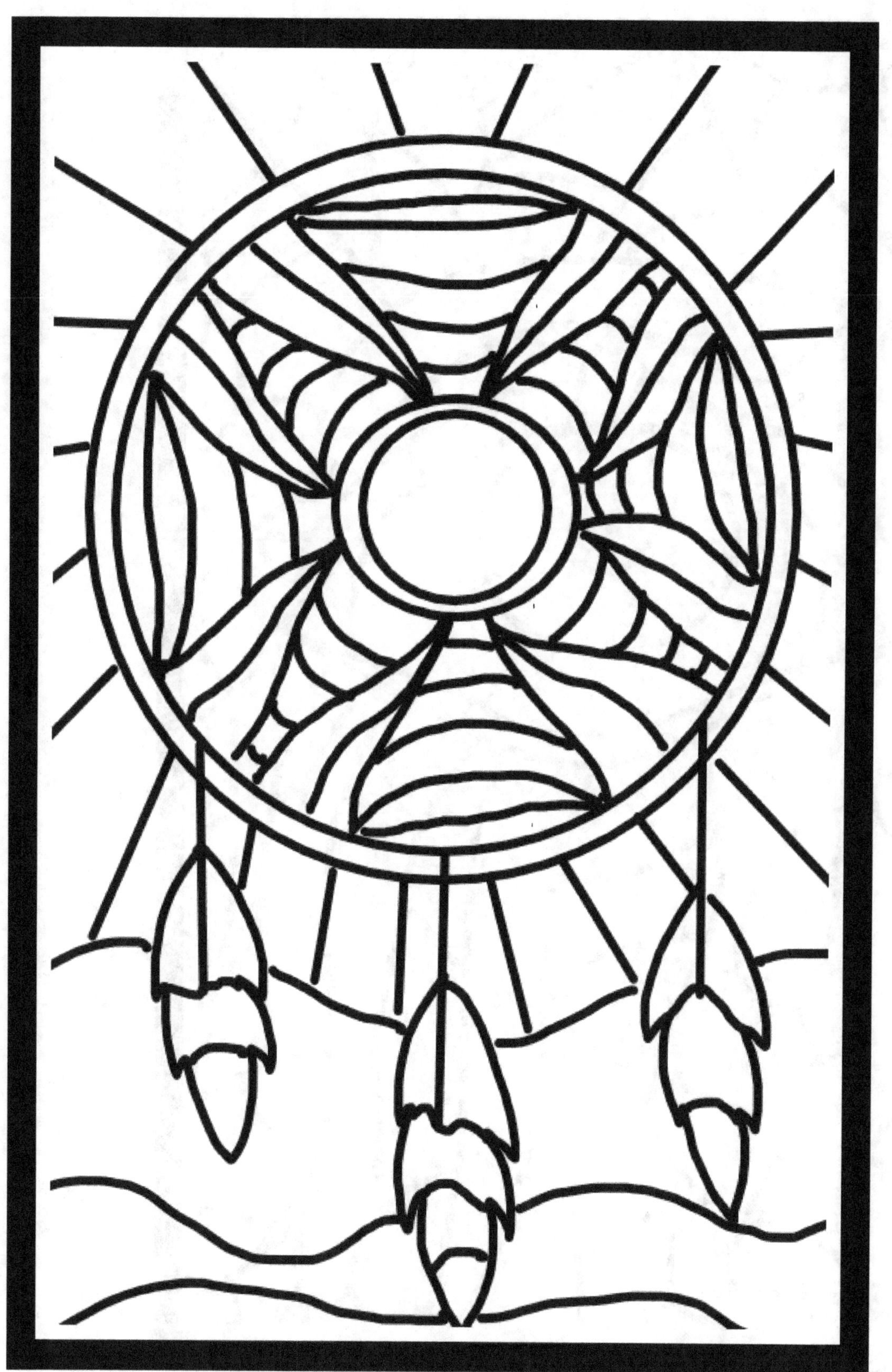

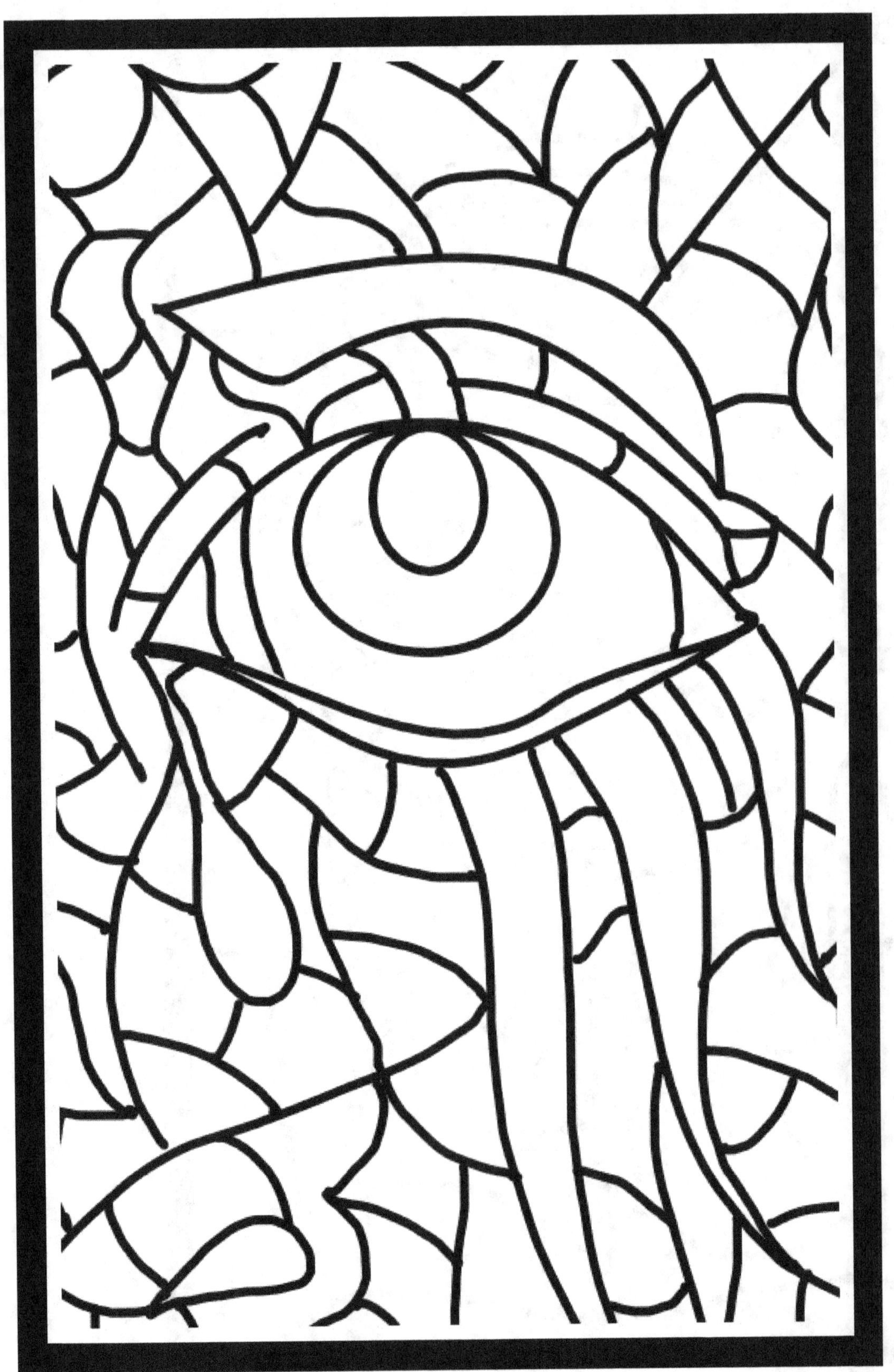

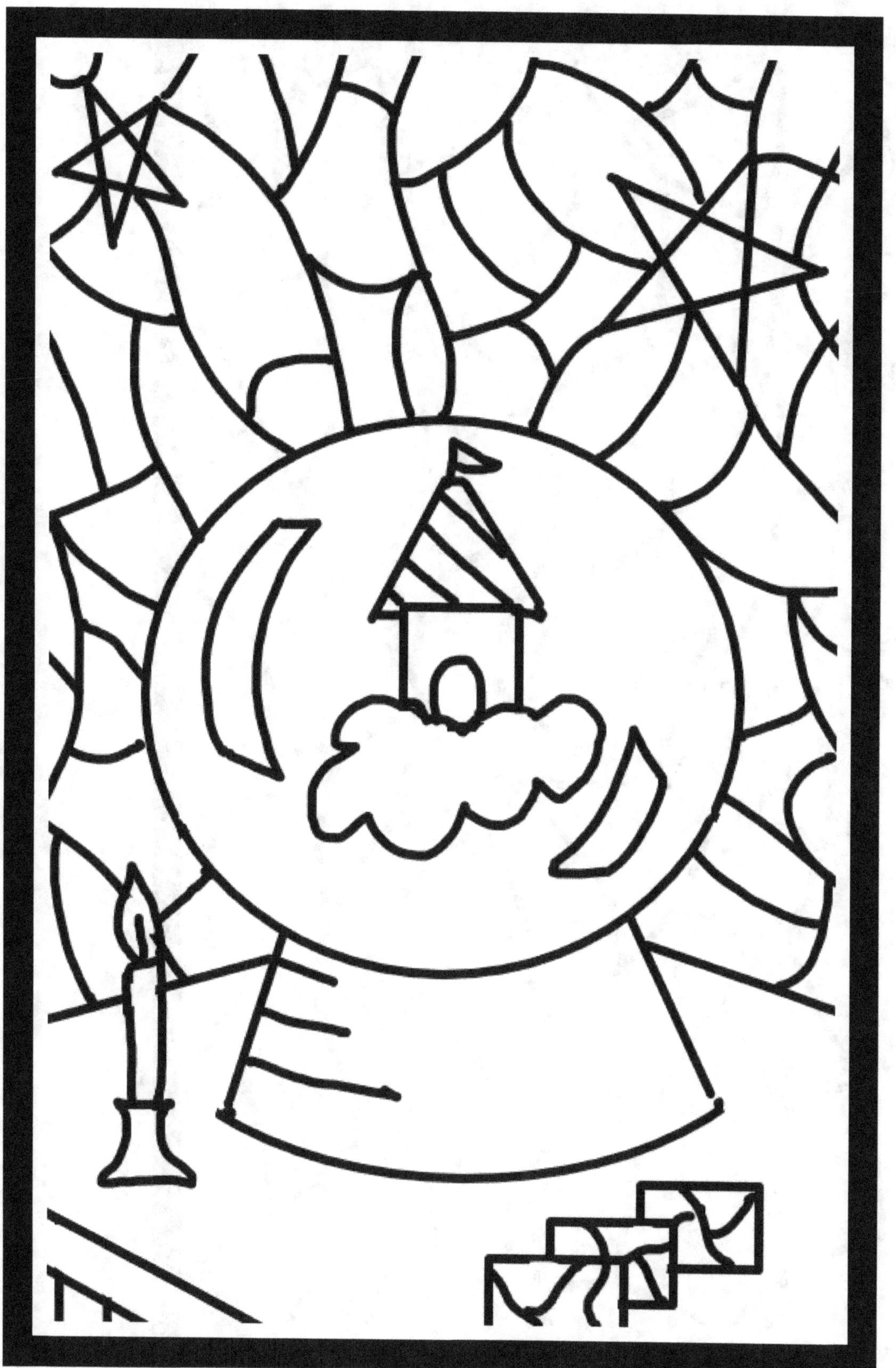

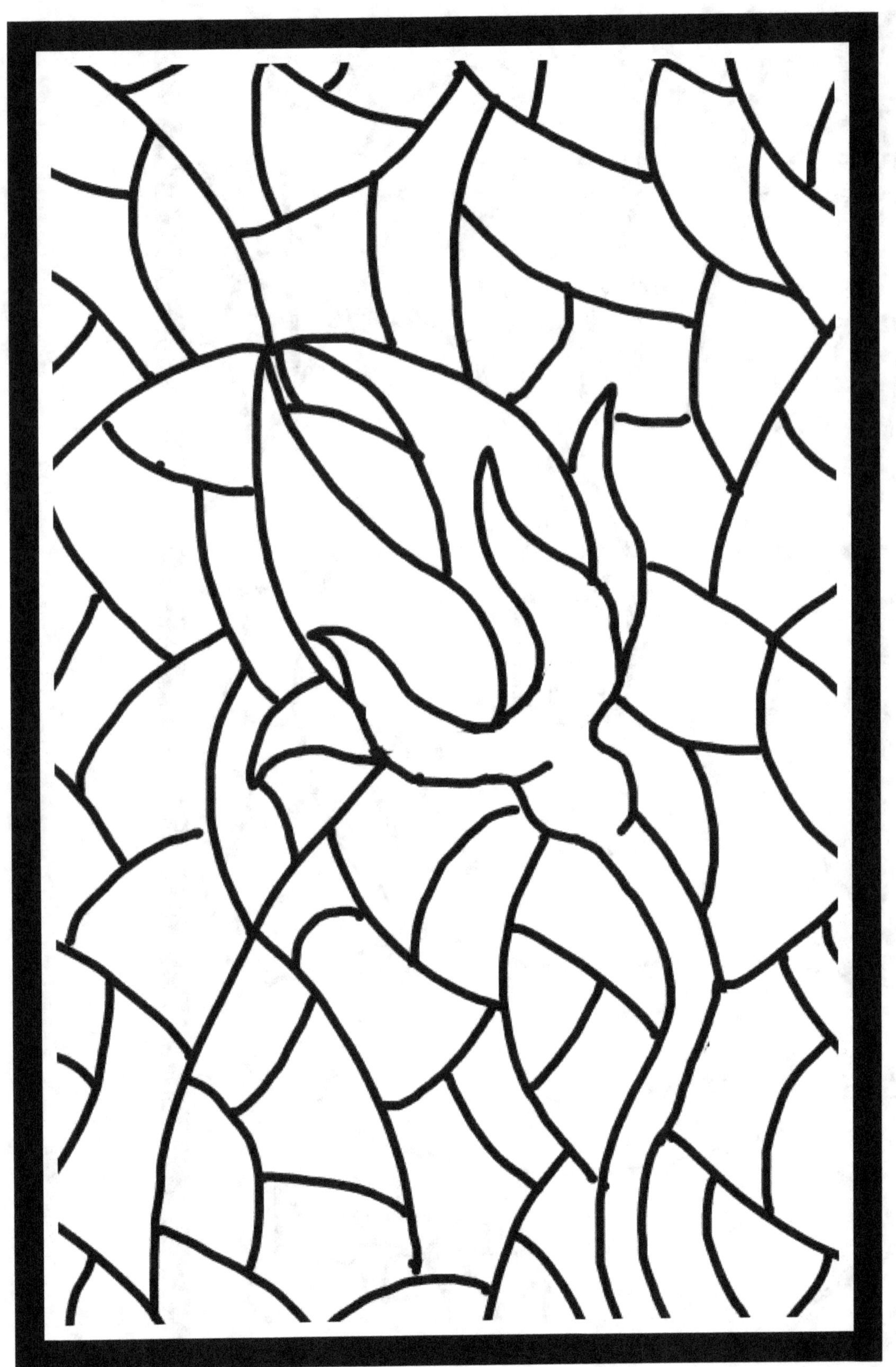

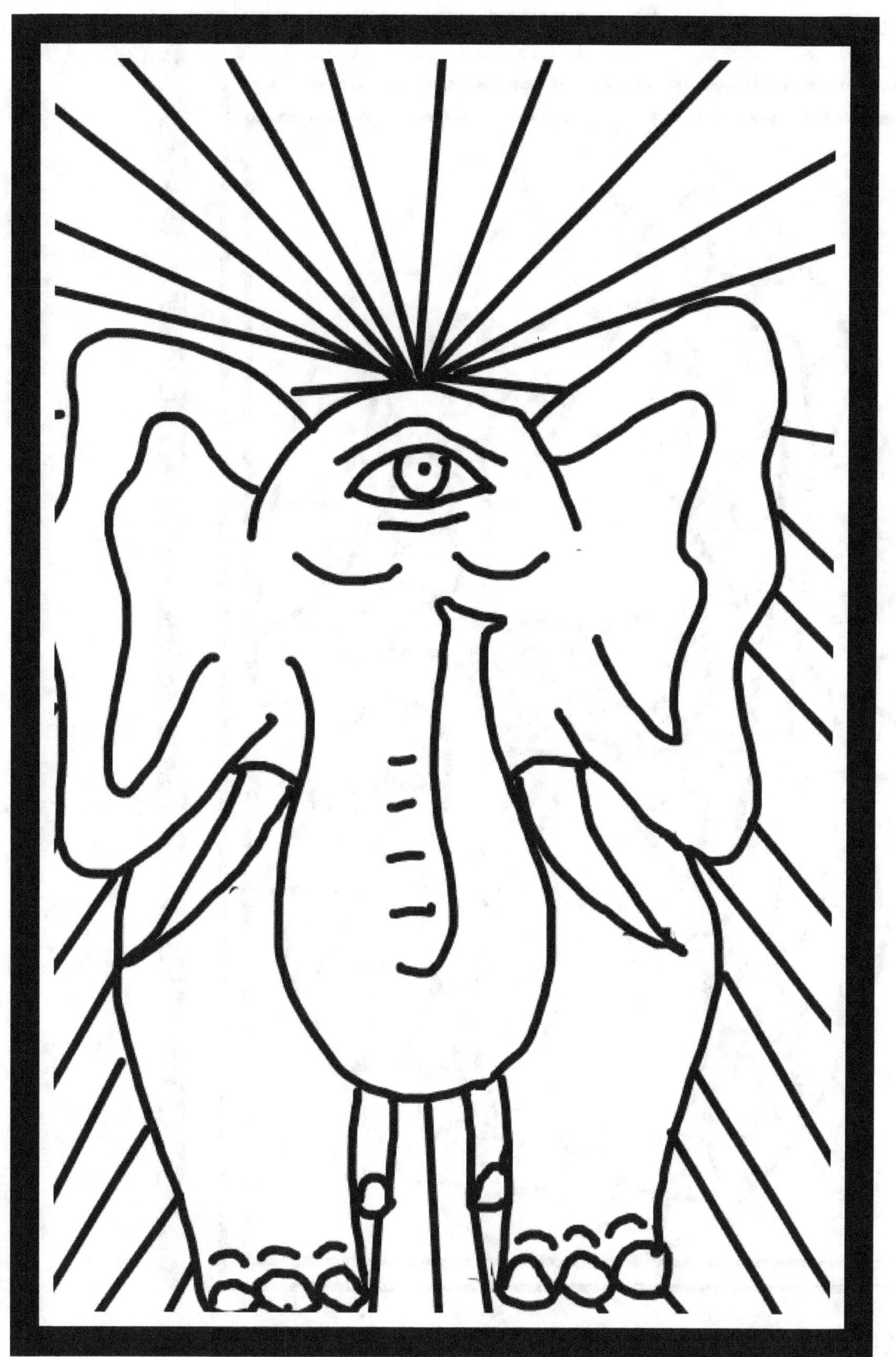

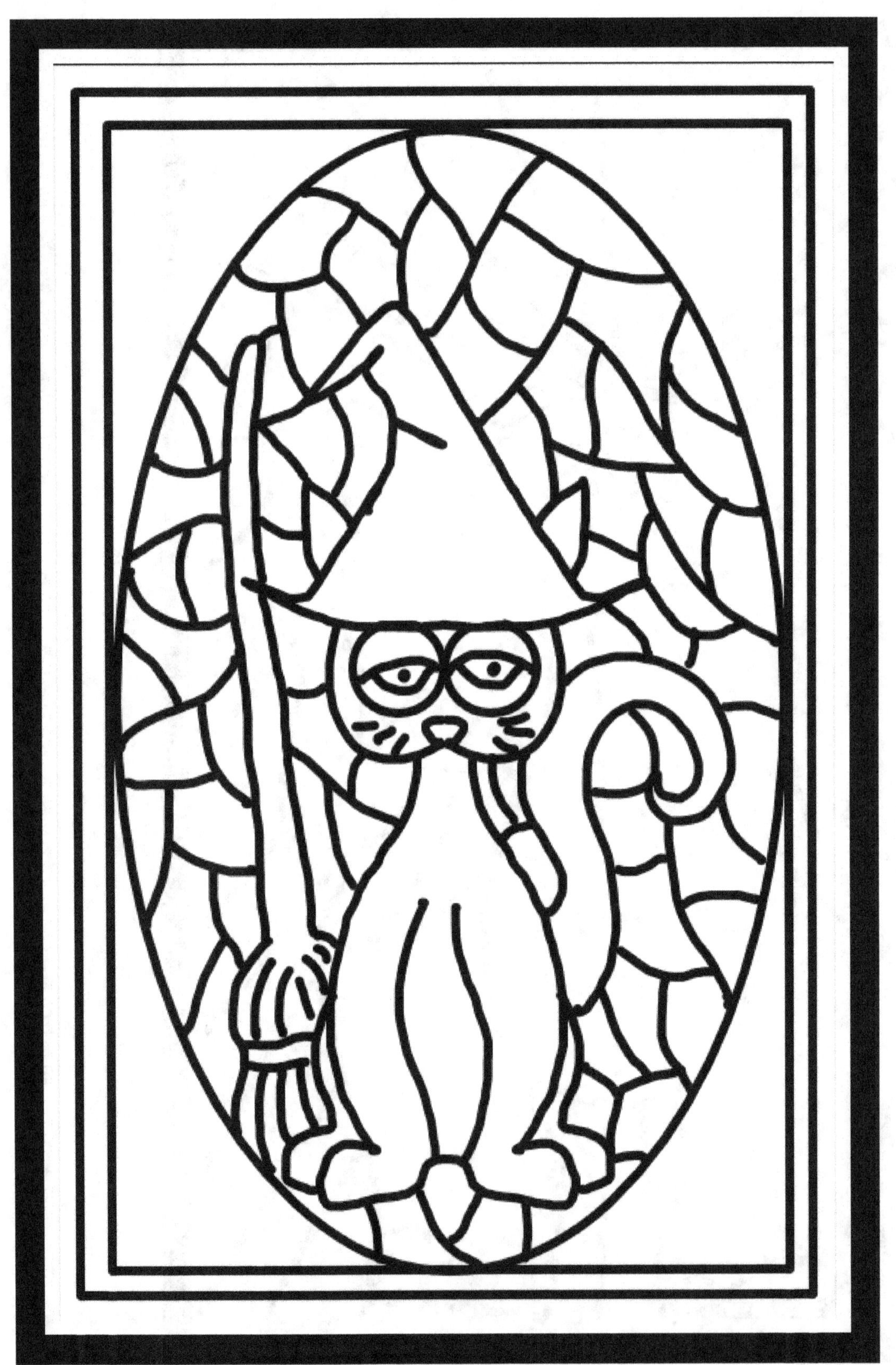

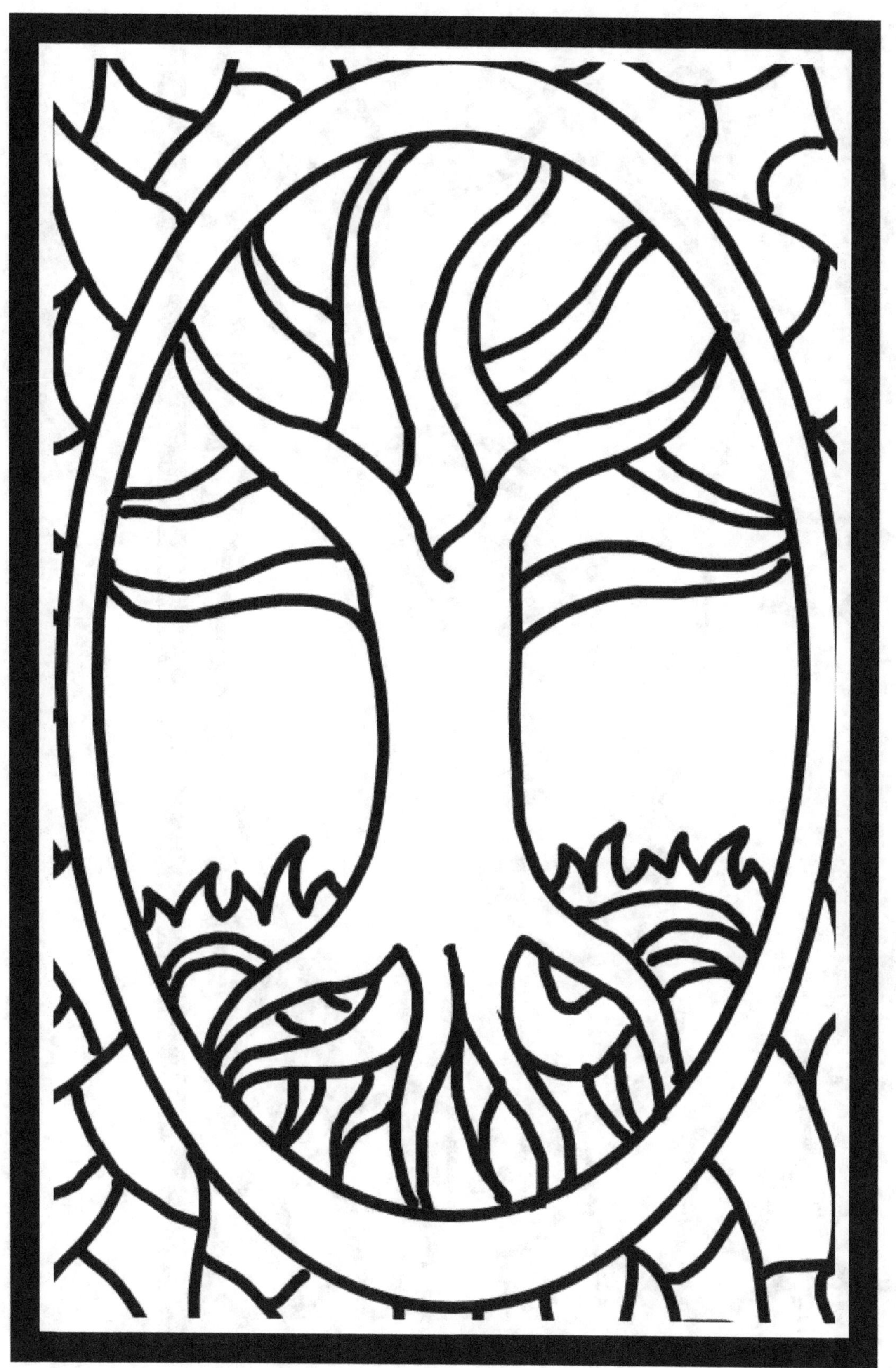

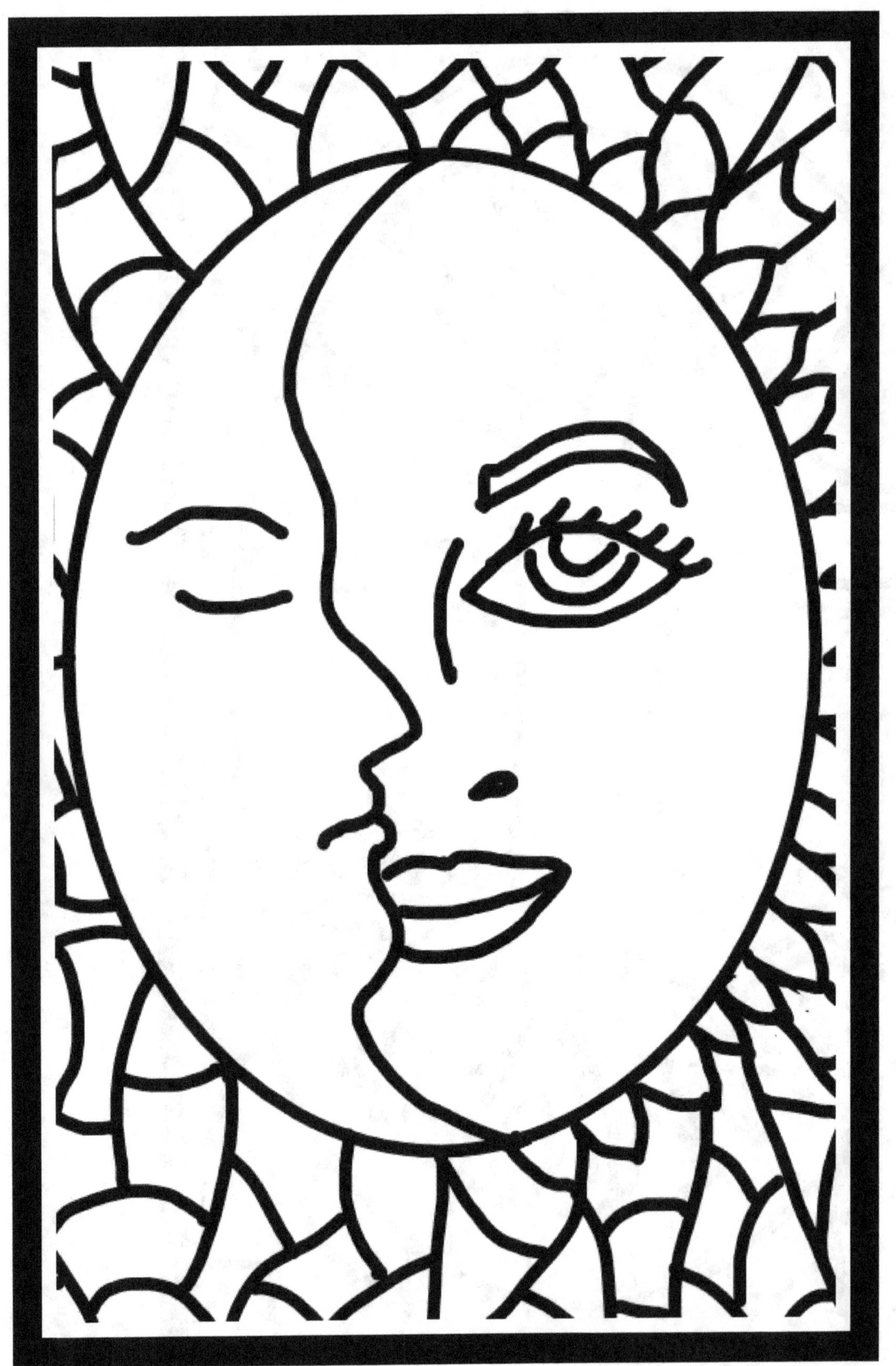

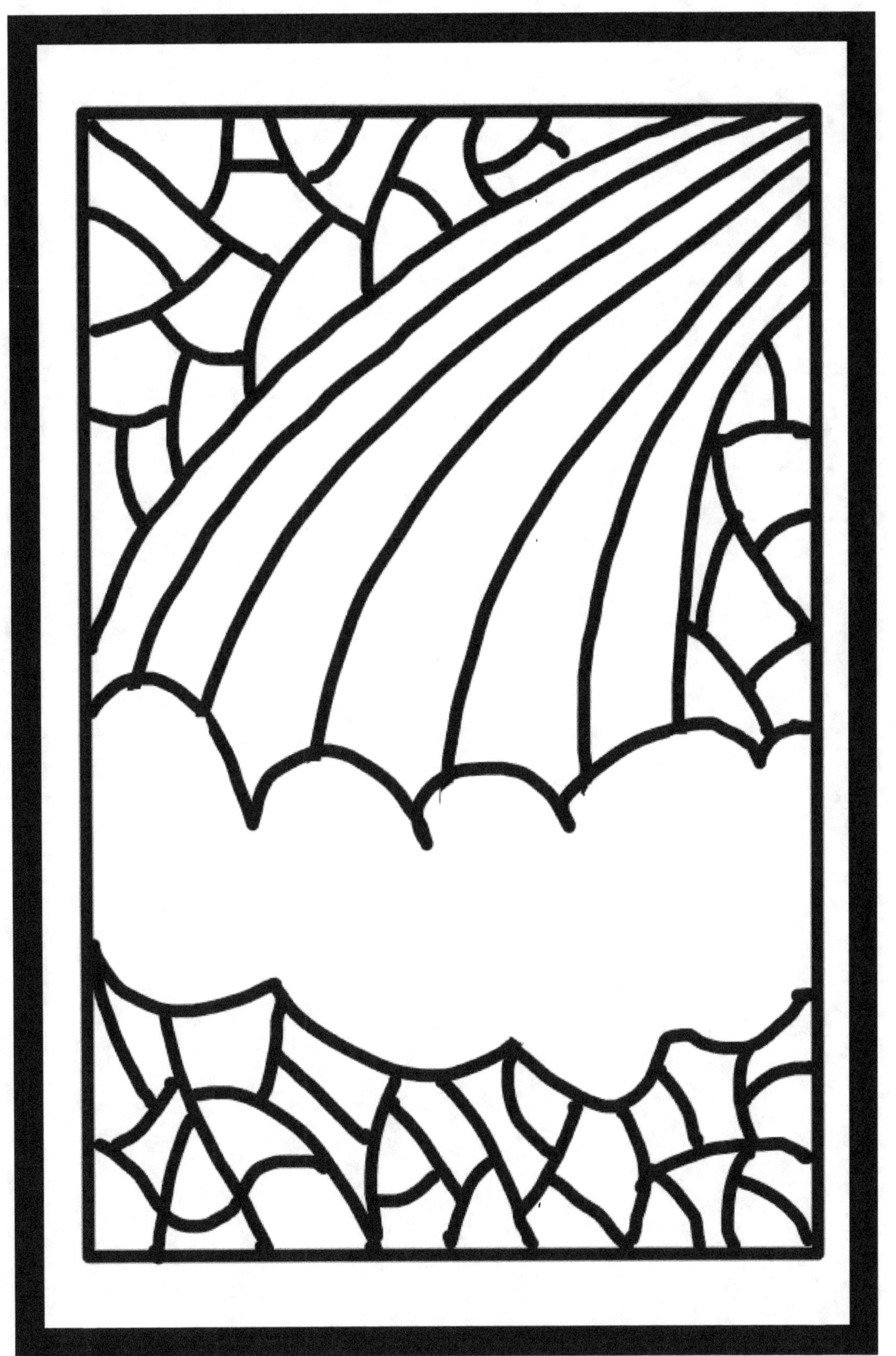